Praise for Fortune's Path and Tom Noser

"Tom iterates on ideas with rigor, making him one of my favorite "thoughtfulls" (yes, two Ls) over the past ten years—whether it's pennant race predictions or debating pricing strategies for enterprise customers."

—Jonas Fridrichsen
Chief Revenue Officer, Meru Health

"Soft skills are critical for product management. This is where the 12 Steps come in. It's an investment in your product org that equips your people to build technology that solves business needs."

—Chris Boyd
Vice President of Product, Built Technologies

"Working with Tom changed the trajectory of my career. Tom helped me find my voice and learn how to use it to advocate for my clients. I never felt like Tom was trying to change me, my perspective, or my approach. He brought his knowledge, experience, and passion for helping people, and partnered with me to leverage my strengths and fine tune my soft skills. In doing so, everyone has benefited—my company, my clients, people in my personal life, and certainly me. I have a newfound confidence and excitement for my career. And I am beyond grateful."

—Tiffany Leader
CloudCME

"We recently landed a five-year deal, and it wouldn't have happened without *Fortune's Path*. We're seeing real improvement on a number of levels."

—Karl Wilkens
Chief Executive Officer & Founder, CloudCME

"*Fortune's Path* provides a solution we can tailor to our specific pain points, with fantastic documentation and some items that we're able to immediately act on. I've already seen some things snap into focus for our team."

—Matt Walker
Product Manager, nContracts

"This is a great book because I'm in it."

—Margaret the pug

Fortune's

PATH

Dear Ben—
You're in the acknowledgement.

You're welcome.
Tom

Fortune's
PATH

12 STEPS TO MANAGE YOUR MOST
IMPORTANT PRODUCT–YOU

TOM NOSER

ILLUSTRATIONS BY DANI LONG & HOLLY CARDEN

Advantage.

Published by Advantage, Charleston, South Carolina.
Member of Advantage Media Group.

ADVANTAGE is a registered trademark, and the Advantage colophon is a trademark of Advantage Media Group, Inc.

Printed in the United States of America.

10 9 8 7 6 5 4 3 2 1

ISBN: 978-1-64225-295-8
LCCN: 2021916658

Cover design by Wesley Strickland.
Layout design by Analisa Smith.

This publication is designed to provide accurate and authoritative information in regard to the subject matter covered. It is sold with the understanding that the publisher is not engaged in rendering legal, accounting, or other professional services. If legal advice or other expert assistance is required, the services of a competent professional person should be sought.

Advantage Media Group is proud to be a part of the Tree Neutral® program. Tree Neutral offsets the number of trees consumed in the production and printing of this book by taking proactive steps such as planting trees in direct proportion to the number of trees used to print books. To learn more about Tree Neutral, please visit **www.treeneutral.com**.

TreeNeutral

Advantage Media Group is a publisher of business, self-improvement, and professional development books and online learning. We help entrepreneurs, business leaders, and professionals share their Stories, Passion, and Knowledge to help others Learn & Grow. Do you have a manuscript or book idea that you would like us to consider for publishing? Please visit **advantagefamily.com**.

For Anna and for my parents. Words will never be enough to say how grateful I am. —Tom

For every fallen scrap of food, every bit of kibble, every entrancing smell, and every patch of sunlight. And for Tom, for sharing the bed. —Margaret the pug

Note:

A version of some material in this book originally appeared online January 30, 2020, as a blog post on the website for Pragmatic Institute and in the Winter 2020 edition of *The Pragmatic*, the quarterly journal of Pragmatic Institute.

Contents

for·tune

| ˈfôrCHən |

noun

1. chance or luck as an external, arbitrary force affecting human affairs: Some malicious act of fortune keeps them separate.

   ▫ luck, especially good luck: This astounding piece of good fortune that has befallen me.

   ▫ (fortunes) the success or failure of a person or enterprise over a period of time or in the course of a particular activity: He is credited with turning around the company's fortunes.

2. a large amount of money or assets: He eventually inherited a substantial fortune.

   ▫ (a fortune) informal a surprisingly high price or amount of money: I spent a fortune on drink and drugs.

Fortune is often found in the path of reason.
—MICHEL DE MONTAIGNE

I already have my fortune. I've always had it.
—MARGARET THE PUG

12 Steps of Product Management

1. Identify what you can and can't control.

2. Improve the things you can control, and accept the things you can't.

3. Make a decision to love your customers.

4. Decide what kind of leader you want to be.

5. Make an inventory of your character.

6. Share your inventory with a trusted friend.

7. Embrace your character—all of it.

8. Make a list of all the people around you who can help you succeed.

9. Speak with all the people on your list to learn what they need to succeed.

10. Take a daily inventory.

11. Improve your insight through contact with customers, colleagues, and people you admire.

12. Carry the messages of customer love and commitment to improvement to everyone you meet.

Foreword

When I was younger, I sometimes wished my father was more like other fathers. Some of my friends had to work tirelessly for their dads to see them as successes—a hearty handshake at graduation was the only semblance of explicit approval they could expect—and part of me thought that was how my relationship with my dad ought to work.

Holding firmly to toxic notions of what a male leader is supposed to look like, I felt in order to truly respect my father, I had to fear him. But I didn't fear him then, and I don't now. How could I? My dad is different. He's emotive, but he doesn't get angry. He's introspective and kind, not brash and cruel. There's no harsh exterior to him, no shell he's created to wall himself off from the world. He means what he says and says what he feels. He rejects the notion that a man is supposed to value cruelty over compassion.

I know now that my dad is strong; it's his sensitivity that makes him so. He's strong not in a broad-shouldered sense, but in a more enduring one—one built out of self-reflection and will. You don't quit drinking and stay sober without an immense amount of willpower and strength.[1] So, when he tells you in this book to make an inventory

---

1   It's not willpower or my own strength that keeps me sober, but thanks, Joe.

of your character, or when he says you should always love your customers, he means it. Take it from me; I've seen it. He worked from home long before it was cool (er, necessary), and since his office is on the same floor as my childhood bedroom, I got a front-row seat to lots of his professional interactions. Not once did I ever hear him get off a call and disparage a client or coworker. If he ever got frustrated, his first response wasn't to judge the source of his frustration, but to self-assess. That response makes him a better businessman, but it also makes him a better person.

Through decades of following the steps he lays out in this book, my father has grown into the strongest, kindest man I've ever known. I still have lots to learn from him. And I'm immensely grateful he's written this book and chosen to share his wisdom with you.

I have no doubt it'll make you better at whatever you choose to do with your life.

—JOE NOSER, MAY 6, 2021

A Note on the Illustrations

Two of my great idols are Michel de Montaigne, a sixteenth-century writer, philosopher, and the inventor of the personal essay, and my seventeen-year-old pug, Margaret.

My idols compared…

	MONTAIGNE	MARGARET
Occupation & family status	Civil servant, writer, philosopher, father	Animal companion, childless
Believed highest form of love is…	Friendship	Friendship
Notable virtue	Endured pain with grace (kidney stones)	Endures pain with grace (arthritis)
Habits	Well-read and intellectually curious	Observant and single-minded
Intellectual disposition	Creative, brilliant, original thinker	Hard to say, but probably a lot like most dogs

My life is spent between these extremes. I have many grand ambitions, but much of the time I'd rather sit in the sun than pursue them. Most people are like that, living between being a genius and being a dog. We are pugs in ruffs, if not to the world, then to ourselves. That's why I've chosen Margaret the pug to be the avatar for those who aspire to practice the 12 Steps of Product Management. If you accept your inner Margaret, you can unlock your inner Montaigne.

Preface

This book is about how to use the principles of recovery to find your fortune. I hope there's a place for love in your fortune. Most of us are afraid to love in business settings. There's no reason to be afraid. If you're just starting your career, or even if you're on your way but feeling stuck, give these principles a try. If you're like me, you'll find more success and be happier for trying.

All of us get to define our fortune. My fortune is a wonderful marriage, raising three children who are smarter than me, living comfortably in a home I love without too much but lacking nothing, loving my customers, podcasting, writing, working with great people in my consultancy Fortune's Path, and learning to love myself. That last one has been hard my whole life. If I love other people first, including the people I work with, it's much easier.

Most of the good stuff in this book comes from other people: my dad, Jamie, John, Chris, Jon, Billy, Mary Frances, Joe, Ted, Michel de Montaigne, and Anna. Always, always Anna.

I also owe a great debt to all the bosses I've had: Frank, Steve, Bryan, Allison, Marjean, Kevin, Eddie, Wes, Robert, Bobby—who was never my boss but always my mentor—and now me. Thanks for believing in me.

Introduction

Each of us must manage the product that is our life. After thirty years of sobriety, I'm happier than I've ever been. I'm a master product manager, podcaster, business owner, writer, father, happy husband, and owner of a noble and virtuous seventeen-year-old dog. Things get better all the time, regardless of my income (mostly). I got this way by applying the disciplines I learned in recovery to every part of my life, and work is a big part of life. I also got this way by defining success for myself. That's what finding your fortune means.

Here's an example that illustrates why you have to know what fortune you're looking for to find it. Imagine you're hard at work on an important announcement when a top-performing salesperson walks into your office. "You busy?" the salesperson asks. "I need something for a giant new customer, and Biggie Cheese says we have to get this done."

What do you do?

How you respond can make or break the next few months of your work life, and maybe even your career. Do you know the right thing to say to land the deal without committing the company to a blank check?

Here's another example. You and your partner haven't been communicating. It's your partner's birthday, and you have reservations at

Chateau Hard-to-Get-into. You're about to leave the office a little early when you get a message from your boss. It's a request for a business plan that will take many hours, and you haven't started because it was supposed to be due in a week. How do you respond?

You can apply the principles of this book to know the right thing to do in both situations. You are not the only customer of the product that is your life. Everyone you know is a customer. Just like with any product, you won't be right for everyone; any product that tries to please everyone inevitably pleases no one. I've made the decision to love my customers. I hope after reading this book, you will too. If you do, you're making the decision to love everyone you meet, no exceptions. Don't think small with your product; we want to create monopoly profits of love. Look for a path that gives you real happiness—not just distraction or amusement—even through trial. That's the path where your fortune is. Value yourself enough to manage yourself and own your effort.[2] Listen for how you can help others, and ask for help yourself. Know that your work and your life are not separate but are not the same either.

When I drank, I craved more alcohol, and I couldn't be satisfied with any amount. For some of us, work is the same way; no matter how hard we work, we always feel empty. I couldn't fix my drinking problem with self-knowledge or willpower. I needed to bring about a personality change through a religious experience. I know "religious" is a loaded word; for me it means something larger than myself. I don't know if there's a God, and if there is one, if he cares about me. I do know there is love, and there is virtue, and I can't have one without the other. Love, virtue, and happiness are learned disciplines. The disciplines I need to stay sober are the same disciplines we need to

---

2   Never say anything is easy, even if it is. You are the most important product you'll ever manage. Don't undersell yourself by saying something is easy.

build virtuous organizations and great products: think about ourselves less, and think of what good we can do for others more. The more we give, the more we get.

Identify What You Can and Can't Control

Not being able to govern events, I govern myself.
—MONTAIGNE

An empty bowl is my responsibility.
—MARGARET THE PUG

We waste a lot of energy working to change things we can't control. To be effective, manage stress, and enjoy life, we need to direct our resources to where they will have the greatest impact. [3] To do this we have to know the difference between things we can control and things we can't.

Let's go back to the scenario in the Introduction. A top-performing salesperson wants your help so he can land a major new deal. What can you control about the situation? You can't control that the salesperson has interrupted you, or that he may believe his work is more important than yours. You can control how you react to the

---

[3] "The advantage of living is not measured by length but by use; some men have lived long, and lived little; attend to it while you are in it." — Montaigne

interruption, which can influence the salesperson, the prospect, and perhaps the direction of your company. That's a lot of power. To use that power well, you need to know where to direct it. I'll go through four choices for how to react to show you how this works:

Imagine you're hard at work when a top-performing salesperson comes into your office. "You busy?" the salesperson asks. "I need to get a new feature into the next release. It's a big opportunity, and Biggie Cheese says we have to get this done."

How should you respond?

- "The next release is already defined."

- "This isn't how we set priorities."

- "What's the opportunity?"

- "I'll talk to Biggie Cheese about it."

"The next release is already defined" may be true, but it's completely unhelpful. Don't use that one. It's selfish and a big reason why businesspeople get frustrated with technical people: correct answers that answer nothing. We'll talk more about the corrupting power of selfishness in Step 3.

"This isn't how we set priorities" is a lot like "The next release is already defined," though it sets you up for a fight with the salesperson because it may not be true. Priorities are always shifting in a business. It's blind thrashing we want to avoid, not reasonable changes in priorities.

"I'll talk to Biggie Cheese about it" is the same thing as saying, "You are not worth my time." It's insulting. It's also impractical, and you're creating more work for yourself. Biggie Cheese may travel or constantly be in meetings. You could wait a long time to get an audience with Biggie Cheese when her representative is right in front of you. "What's the opportunity?" is the only reasonable answer if what you're working on is anything other than an emergency. Accept that the salesperson interrupted you. You can't control that. You can make the best choice for how you react.

You

Look at the list below and decide how you think of each item. Do you have control of it, can you influence it, or do you have no control? Put a √ in the column that describes how you feel about attitude, effort, schedule, and what you do next.

TABLE 1: ATTITUDE, EFFORT, SCHEDULE, AND PRIORITY

	I can control	I can influence	I have no control
My attitude			
My effort			
My schedule			
My priorities: what I do next			

Attitude, effort, schedule, and priorities—what you do next—depend on each other. If meetings and correspondence overwhelm your schedule, your attitude and effort will suffer, and you won't be able to work on your priorities. If you can't prioritize your own work, you'll feel micromanaged, your effort will suffer, and you may not put in the hours you need to succeed.

Other People

What about other people can you influence? What can you control? Do the same thing you did above, and put a √ in the column that best describes how you feel about each item.

TABLE 2: WHAT I CONTROL ABOUT OTHER PEOPLE

	I can control	I can influence	I have no control
Other people's attitudes			
Other people's effort			
How other people do their work			
Supplying the information other people need to do their jobs			

You can always influence another person's attitude, but it can take a long time to see results. Typically, you need to improve someone's attitude before you see their effort improve. You can ruin someone's effort if you damage their attitude. That can be done in no time. We'll

> Information is power. Wisdom—knowing what to do with information—is a superpower.

talk more about your ability to influence other people's effort and attitude in Step 4. You can never control someone's attitude; we are all free in our minds.

You can both influence and control how other people do their work, but you shouldn't. How other people do their work is none of your business as long as they do it legally and ethically. The quality of their work and the results of their work might be your vital concern, but how they do the work is for them to manage within the law.

If you can supply information other people need to do their jobs, you should. Collecting, organizing, interpreting, and sharing information with others is one of the surest ways to rise to prominence in an organization. Information is power. Wisdom—knowing what to do with information—is a superpower.

Your Organization

Take a look at this list and identify what you're responsible for in your organization. Then decide if you can control it, influence it, or have no control. Put an *X* in the appropriate column. (Most of my work has been in the software business, and this list reflects that, but it's still pretty applicable to most businesses.)

TABLE 3: RESPONSIBILITY, CONTROL & INFLUENCE

	I'm responsible	I can control	I can influence	I have no control
Strategy: What big things is your organization trying to achieve?				
Prioritization: What should be done, when should it be done, and how much effort should be expended on it?				
Market research: Competitive analysis, customer understanding, etc.				
Product design: What is the product, and how does it work?				
Pricing: How much do we charge, and what discounts are available?				
Revenue growth: Finding new customers, growing existing customers, and preventing customers from leaving				
Customer experience: Implementation, support, adoption, loyalty, and reputation				

If you have more than three *X*s in the "I'm responsible" column, you need to delegate more. If you have any rows where you checked both "I'm responsible" and "I have no control," you need to either get rid of responsibility or gain control. If you have responsibility for many things but little control, that's unhealthy. Interdisciplinary functions like product management and marketing are vulnerable to the responsibility-without-control dilemma. We all have to influence and lead to get things done, but some of us have to do this more than others.

It's possible for something to start out as a "no control" item at the start of your career and grow into something you can influence or even control completely. NBA rookie salaries are set by their draft order. They have little control over their pay in their first year. As they improve, they get more control and can demand more, but there are limits. Even LeBron James can't demand $10 billion a year when the total revenue for the league is about $9 billion.

Chapter in a Chart: Identify What You Can and Can't Control

Things you can't control ➤	Things you can
The weather	What you bring on a journey
The distance between two destinations	When you leave
What other people put on their websites	What you respond to
	What you ignore
Who enters your market	How you position yourself against competitors
Who you fall in love with	How you treat the people you love

Why it matters	What to do about it
Napoleon lost over 400,000 men because he couldn't control how far Moscow is from Paris and when it gets cold in Russia.	Take collaboration seriously. Seek and give input freely. I doubt all of Napoleon's men thought invading Russia was a great idea.
When Google started, it couldn't control how people built their websites. It could control how it ranked websites in searches and which websites it included in results.	Stick to your own model. I'm quite sure some website owners didn't like how Google ranked them when Google started, and I doubt Google did much to respond to them.
I worked for a software company that competed against giant rivals. We chose one market—healthcare—to make our stand. It was our life. It was just another vertical to the big boys. By focusing on what we could control—getting to know one market—and accepting what we couldn't—who came into our market—we built a dominant market share, beating organizations four hundred times our size.	Keep your focus on things you can control. Don't worry about things you can't.
I fell in love with a woman almost eight years older than me. For us, love isn't about making accommodations; it's about making each other happy.	You may need to do some things before you're ready, and you may need to wait longer than you'd like for others. Try not to mind it too much. Thinking about what's good for others helps.

Each chapter has exercises to help you put the principles of the step you just read into practice. You'll read a story based on a real-world situation and be presented with a choice. What you choose will affect what happens next and the outcome of the story. Different choices lead to different outcomes. Use what you learned in the chapter to get the best result, and if you don't get the best result, try again and apply the principles from the chapter you just read. The scenarios aren't tests; they're practice, and practice is about repetition, so try them more than once.

Practice Step 1

Hint: "You have to understand what you can and cannot control to succeed and be happy."

The scenario:

You've been assigned to lead a project that's critical for your organization. The deadline is two months out, and you think it will be a simple project. The chief revenue officer (CRO) is the executive sponsor. You've scheduled the project kickoff meeting with the team and the CRO. The CRO's schedule is a nightmare, so just getting the meeting on the calendar feels like a victory. You have a general idea about the project, but you and the CRO have not been able to get together to go over things in detail yet. You log into the meeting a few minutes early so you can greet the team as they come in. Just then you get a text from the CRO: "Can't make the meeting. Go on without me."

What do you do next?

If you want to …

⊛ Reschedule the meeting for a time when the CRO can make it, go to page 17.

⊛ Have the meeting without the CRO, go to page 21.

RESCHEDULE THE MEETING FOR A TIME WHEN THE CRO CAN MAKE IT.

As folks log in, you tell them that the CRO needs to be at the kickoff, and since he can't make it, there's no point in having the meeting. People are relieved to have the time back.

You send the CRO a note saying you're rescheduling the meeting because he needs to be there. While you're looking on his calendar to reschedule, you get a response from the CRO: "I told you to go on without me." You feel like you need to be firm; it's best to start the project off right. You send a response: "You're the project sponsor. You need to be at the kickoff to explain the critical success factors to the team. I'm rescheduling."

You find a time two weeks out. You're not too worried because it should be a simple project.

Two weeks pass by, and the team gets back together for the rescheduled kickoff. After everyone joins the meeting, you waste some awkward time waiting for the CRO. At ten minutes past the start time of the meeting, the CRO is a no-show, although he accepted the meeting, and it's on his calendar. You send him a text with a link to join the meeting. Five more minutes pass, and you finally get a response: "Meeting never got on my calendar. Go on without me." You read the CRO's message to the team. The lead developer sighs. "Well, we've wasted two weeks, and we're in exactly the spot we were two weeks ago. I'm going to tell my boss we can't make this deadline." He exits the meeting.

Yikes! How did this happen?

You need to accept that the CRO won't be involved much. He may be the executive sponsor, but you need to be the leader. Step in and lead.

Good leaders don't wait for direction from above when they have a team in front of them that needs direction. You should have had the original kickoff meeting and explained the project as best you could. At least that way the team could have done some investigation while waiting for more clarity from the CRO.

HAVE THE MEETING
WITHOUT THE CRO.

You explain the project to the team as best you can. You explain that the CRO is hard to get ahold of, but you'll take care of that for the team.

The lead developer asks if you have any details about what data needs to be shared between the systems. You don't yet. He says he'll send you documentation about what data your system can share, and you can start with that. The junior dev says he found documentation about the partner's API, and he'll start reading through it.

You create a project schedule that assumes the CRO won't make any of the meetings. Instead, you'll send him email updates about project status. You look over the API documentation the lead developer gave you, and it looks like any data the partner might need is available. Even though the project isn't due for two months, you tell the team you want to have daily virtual check-ins to monitor progress and impediments.

The next day you send a note to the team telling them you looked over the API documentation, and you don't have any questions for now. None of the other team members respond except the junior developer, who says he looked at the partner's API documentation, and it's pretty weak. He says you're going to need to get one of their developers on a meeting to know how to proceed.

What do you do next?

Read "Step 2: Improve the Things You Can Control, and Accept the Things You Can't" to find out.

WHAT COMES NEXT

Knowing what you can and can't control is critical to finding success in work and happiness in life. Spend your energy on things where you can make a difference. Let go of things you can't control. It's simple, but often it's not easy, and if you want happiness and peace of mind, you have to do it. The next chapter is about how to take charge of what you can and let go of what you can't.

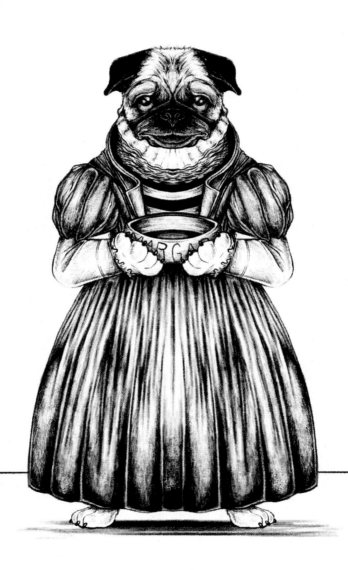

STEP 2

Improve the Things You Can Control, and Accept the Things You Can't

The Emperor Vespasian, though sick with the sickness that killed him, did not stop wanting to know about the state of the Empire, and even in bed never stopped dispatching many affairs of importance. And when his physician scolded him for doing something harmful to his health, he said: 'An emperor must die standing.' That is a fine statement, and worthy of a great prince.
—MONTAIGNE

I can't open the peanut butter jar, but I know who can.
—MARGARET THE PUG

It's courageous to accept that you're dying and not give up on living. It's also humble, just like asking someone to open a jar for you is humble. We need humility and courage to take command of what we can control and accept what we can't. Attitude, effort, schedule, and prioritization are the foundation. They're essential to control, and they can always be improved.

Let's look at an example.

You have a dinner date scheduled with your romantic partner for their birthday. The reservation is for a hot new restaurant that's difficult to get into. The two of you have been stressed out and not communicating lately. You've both been looking forward to dinner so you can get back on track. You're about to leave the office when you receive an email from your boss. The subject is "Need this by 9 tomorrow." It's a request for a report she wants to share with the CEO when they meet to discuss next year's budget. You have to collect and summarize a lot of data from many different sources because she's making a pitch for the CEO to invest in your group. Her meeting got moved up a week because the CEO has to travel unexpectedly.

You don't have a template to work from, but you've talked with your boss about the report, and you have a good idea of what she wants. It could be five or six hours of work.

What should you do?

- Call your partner and tell them you have to reschedule because you need to work late.

- Go to dinner with your partner as scheduled.

- Ask your partner if they want to hang out with you while you write the report. You can get takeout.

If you call your partner and reschedule, you'll make a bad situation worse. In a choice between who you love more—your partner or yourself—you're choosing yourself. If you ask your partner to get takeout and be with you while you work, you've made your problem their problem. The only right thing to do is to go to dinner as scheduled. You should accept that your partner only has one birthday a year, and today's the day. You need to honor your commitment. You also need to accept that you have a commitment to your boss. You can't control that schedules got changed, and you ended up with two commitments you need to honor in one night. Today is about your partner, so it looks like you're pulling an all-nighter.

You

Let's look back at your chart from the first step. Add a space below for why you feel the way you do about your attitude, your effort, your schedule, and what you do next.

TABLE 4: WHY DO I FEEL THIS WAY?

	I can control	I can influence	I have no control
My attitude			
Why do I feel this way?			
My effort			
Why do I feel this way?			

	I can control	I can influence	I have no control
My schedule			
Why do I feel this way?			
What I do next			
Why do I feel this way?			

This space is where the work happens. Take ten solid minutes to think about why you feel the way you do. Write it out for all four items: attitude, effort, schedule, and priorities. Write whatever comes to mind without judging what you're writing. Maybe you feel like you can't control your attitude because you've been getting bad results. You can still take pride in things like your approach, your discipline, your growing competence, and your professionalism. A good attitude doesn't mean you feel good; it means you're open to the possibility that something good can come from your current situation. You need to divorce your attitude from results to master your attitude. If you wait for better results to improve your attitude, you may wait a long time, and as soon as results get worse, so will your attitude.

Look at what you wrote. See how the items—attitude and effort, schedule and priorities—are related to each other. Attitude and effort are two sides of one coin. Attitude is mental, and effort is physical. Like attitude, effort should be divorced from results. Effort often falters when we feel unappreciated. Other people's appreciation of our effort is unimportant. Only you know if you gave something your best. Control your effort so you can control your self-respect. Spend your effort on things that create value. Many things that take a lot of effort are of little value. An igneous rock can take a million years to make, but nobody is storing them up for a rainy day. Some things that take no effort—such as saying thank you—are invaluable in the right circumstance.

> A good attitude doesn't mean you feel good; it means you're open to the possibility that something good can come from your current situation.

Controlling your schedule may seem impossible, but it's not. You can always say no; you just might not be able to say no without consequences. In college I organized my schedule around drinking. I'd pick classes that started after noon because getting up before noon was hard when I went to bed at three. 3 a.m. emails can be like a drinking binge: we do it because we can't help ourselves. Not true. I never have to drink again, and you never have to write another 3 a.m. email.

What you do next is the other side of your schedule. Unless you're an addict, you have free will. You can always choose what you do next. Even if you're an addict, you can recover and get your free will back.

Other People

Let's look at your chart about other people from Step 1 again. Just like you did before, add a space below, "Why do I think this?" and do some more truthful writing.

TABLE 5: WHAT I CONTROL ABOUT OTHER PEOPLE

	I can control	I can influence	I have no control
Other people's attitudes			
Why do I think this?			
Other people's effort			
Why do I think this?			

	I can control	I can influence	I have no control
How other people do their work			
Why do I think this?			
Supplying the information other people need to do their jobs			
Why do I think this?			

You're crazy if you think you can control everyone's attitude. You're a coward if you think you can't influence anyone's attitude. Leadership is how you influence other people's attitudes, effort, and how they do their work. You can start to lead by supplying information people need to do their work.

> Leadership is how you influence other people's attitudes, effort, and how they do their work.

31

Let's look again at the story of the interrupting salesperson.

Imagine you're hard at work when a top-performing salesperson comes into your office. "You busy?" the salesperson asks. "I need to get a new feature into the next release. It's a big opportunity, and Biggie Cheese says we have to get this done."

"What's the opportunity?" you ask.

"This thing will make my year," the salesperson says. "And it's a takeaway from our biggest competitor. What they want us to do is super simple."

How should you respond?

⊛ "Wow! That sounds awesome!"

⊛ "What do they want done?"

⊛ "Thanks. I'll follow up with Biggie Cheese."

This is a perfect opportunity to influence what the salesperson does next. If you say, "What do they want done?" you'll sound like you're being skeptical. Salespeople hate that. Instead, get on their side and act excited even if you have to fake it. Say, "Wow! That sounds awesome," and see what the salesperson says next. You might be able to give the salesperson the information they need without having to do much work.

Your Organization

Block out time for thinking, research, and writing. Put those times on your calendar. Treat each time like an appointment, and don't violate it. Create office hours when you're available for *ad hoc* conversations. If you establish regular office hours, you have good reason to push people off when they interrupt you outside of office hours. Attend every meeting, accept every invitation, return every email, and you'll be a responsive wreck, or you'll work eighty hours a week, and that's just as bad. Don't forget it's your schedule. You should own it and control it.[4] To paraphrase Jimi Hendrix, you're the one who has to die when it's your turn to die. So live your life the way you want to.

When you get interrupted, perform some quick triage with a prioritization criterion. Here's an example:

- Work that makes you smarter about your customers

- Work required to keep a promise

- Work that will delight customers

- Work that will make you rich

These priorities trump each other. If something will make you smarter about your customers, don't worry about getting rich from it. Same for customer delight—if it will delight customers and it's responsible, do it.

---

4   Recognize when your desire to control becomes insubordination. Don't undermine organizational goals and call it constructive criticism.

Chapter in a Chart: Improve the Things You Can Control, and Accept the Things You Can't

Things you can control	Things you can't control
Your attitude	The results of what you do
Your effort	How other people interpret your effort
Your schedule	Interruptions
Your priorities, or what you do next	Other people's ideas of what your priorities should be
Your definition of success	How others define success

Why it matters	What to do about it
Attitude has to be separated from results because so much affects results that's out of our control. Attitude is just another word for commitment; I'm committed to staying positive, or I'm a knucklehead.	Take pride in your professionalism. When you feel down, read your résumé. Look at your LinkedIn connections. Pull up some work you're proud of. Call somebody who loves you.
At the start of his Hall of Fame career, Ken Griffey Jr. smiled a lot while playing baseball. Some people didn't think he was trying hard enough because he smiled so much. By the end of his career, Ken didn't smile so much anymore. Only you know if you gave something your best effort. Your best effort won't be the same every time.	Cut yourself some slack when you're stressed or feeling low. Shake yourself up if you know you need to give more effort.
Lincoln didn't plan to get shot at Ford's Theatre. Interruptions happen, sometimes terrible ones. How we deal with them is what matters. Andrew Johnson, Lincoln's successor, was a terrible president partly because of his desire to exact revenge for Lincoln's death.	Don't let interruptions derail your priorities.
Saving the Union was Lincoln's top priority, not freeing the slaves, despite the pleas of abolitionists. Eventually, freeing the slaves became central to Lincoln's plan to save the Union.	Always listen. Sometimes other people are right about what our priorities should be.
Meaning is more important than money. Once you've fulfilled your basic needs and comforts, in the absence of meaning, money only buys distraction.	Decide how much money you need to live. Over about $75,000 a year, money can be a game of diminishing returns. Under $50,000 a year, and it's hard to survive.

Practice Step 2

Hint: "You can control more than you think, but you're trying to control the wrong things."

The scenario:

You're leading a critical integration project with a partner. The chief revenue officer (CRO) is the executive sponsor for the project. You held the project kickoff meeting with your team without the CRO because the CRO is too busy to come to any of your meetings.

After the kickoff meeting, you looked over the documentation for integrations your lead developer sent you, and you don't have any questions for now. The junior developer says he looked at the partner's documentation, and it's not very helpful. He says you're going to need to get one of the partner's developers on a meeting to know how to proceed.

What should you do next?

If you want to ...

⊛ Send a note to the CRO asking for a contact at the partner, go to page 39.

⊛ Send a note to the lead developer asking if they could look over the partner's API documentation, go to page 41.

SEND A NOTE TO THE CRO ASKING FOR A CONTACT AT THE PARTNER.

You write the CRO a note he can forward to everyone on the project, both on your side and at the partner. You identify your team members, their roles, and their contact information. You ask the partner to do the same for their side. Shortly after you send the note to the CRO, you get a response.

"Thanks for this. Forwarded." There's no other information, but you have the email address of the CRO's contact at the partner, along with your note forwarded without comment. Some quick Google sleuthing of the partner's email address shows you she's a senior vice president (SVP) for partnerships.

What should you do next?

If you want to …

⚜ Write a note to the CRO describing your understanding of the project—why it's important to both companies, what the affected products are, who the affected users are, and some guesses about acceptance criteria for the integration, go to page 45.

⚜ Wait for someone at the partner to get back to you, go to page 43.

SEND A NOTE TO THE LEAD DEVELOPER ASKING IF THEY COULD LOOK OVER THE PARTNER'S API DOCUMENTATION.

You send your note, but you don't hear anything back. The next day you have your virtual check-in as usual. No one shows up. You send another note to the lead developer asking where they are. You get a response. "This project has no executive sponsor. I'm not wasting my time on it."

Yikes. How did this happen?

The project has an executive sponsor; he just happens to be mostly unavailable. You're going to have to clarify things and make decisions as if you were the executive sponsor, but do it in a way where you don't exceed your authority or make anyone look bad, particularly the CRO.

The project has a lot of things you can't control, like the executive sponsor's availability or the lead developer's attitude. You can control your effort. The project is going to be a lot of work because leadership is always a lot of work, and you need to be this project's leader.

Go back to "Practice Step 2" on page 37 and try again.

WAIT FOR SOMEONE AT THE PARTNER TO GET BACK TO YOU. YOU DON'T WANT TO WASTE EFFORT ASSUMING TOO MUCH.

A few days go by. You've stopped doing the daily check-ins with the team because nothing has changed. No one from the partner has gotten back to you. You send another note to the CRO, saying you need a technical contact at the partner for the project. You hear nothing. In frustration you send an email to the SVP at the partner, asking for the name of a technical contact. You hear nothing. You're about to forget the whole project when you get an email from your boss.

"CRO has asked me to take you off the partnership integration project. What gives?"

Yikes. How did this happen?

The CRO can't be actively involved, but you can't forget about him either. Waiting for the partner to contact you is too passive, and sending a note directly to the SVP at the partner is too aggressive. You need to go through the CRO. He owns the relationship with the partner.

Make a list of everyone who can help you succeed on this project and talk to them about what they need to succeed. We'll talk about how to do this in Steps 8 and 9.

Go back to "Practice Step 2" on page 37 and try again.

WRITE A NOTE TO THE CRO DESCRIBING YOUR UNDERSTANDING OF THE PROJECT.

You write a note to your CRO. In the note you describe your understanding of why the integration is important to both companies, what the affected products are, who the affected users are, and some guesses about acceptance criteria for the integration. You format the note so the CRO can easily skim it. You want to add a clear call to action so the CRO will know what to do next.

What should your call to action be? Read "Step 3: Make a Decision to Love Your Customers" to find out.

WHAT COMES NEXT

There's one exception to the "Accept what you can't control" rule: how other people treat us. We can't control it, but we can influence it, and we don't have to accept it. A great way to protect yourself from other people's bad behavior is to love them no matter what. The next chapter is about making a decision to love your customers. Here's a hint: love isn't what you think.

Make a Decision to Love Your Customers

*What cannot be done by reason, and by wisdom
and by skill, is never done by force.*
—MONTAIGNE

I always love Tom, even when I'm messing the rug.
—MARGARET THE PUG

"Fake it until you make it" is one of the most powerful ideas I've learned in recovery. It means actions are more important than motivations. It's not enough to say we love customers or even feel love for customers. We have to act like we love customers. Love in business means a passion to know the other, a willingness to sacrifice, honesty with courtesy, kindness, anticipation, and a fair exchange of value. It also means clearly seeing what needs to be done and having the courage to do it. Our greatest protection against bad people is to love them as they are. You won't be fooled by thinking you can change them.

Let's go back to our story to see this in action.

Imagine you're hard at work when a top-performing salesperson comes into your office. "You busy?" the salesperson asks. "I need to get a new feature into the next release. It's a big opportunity, and Biggie Cheese says we have to get this done."

"What's the opportunity?" you ask.

"This thing will make my year," the salesperson says. "And it's a takeaway from our biggest competitor. What they want us to do is super simple."

"Wow! That sounds awesome!"

"Yeah, this thing will either make my year or get me fired," says the salesperson. "I have a call with the prospect in five minutes."

"Mind if I sit in on the call?" you ask.

"I don't mind," says the salesperson, "as long as you don't talk about the product. It's the wrong time for that. If you want to say anything, write it down, and show me first."

How do you respond?

- "If you don't trust me to talk, I shouldn't be in the meeting."

- "We should get on the call."

- "If we're going to work together, we need to respect each other."

If you think about yourself first, you'll mess this one up. We have an obligation to give love before being loved. It's like raising kids. We want to see our customers flourish and grow. We protect our customers, educate them, and treat them with compassion. Customers may be immature, but they're more likely smart, skilled, driven, and anxious. Since this opportunity will either make the salesperson's year or get him fired, he's probably anxious. Now is not the time to call out his silly comment about not wanting you to talk. Come back to that later; right now, the call with the prospect is more important. When you do come back to the comment about not talking, ask the salesperson why he said that before you defend yourself. The comment may have nothing to do with you.

You

I used to get angry with people when they wouldn't do what I wanted. Today, getting angry feels like a waste. I have little lasting tension in my marriage because I don't think much about what Anna can do for me, and I enjoy doing things for her. It makes me happy to make Anna happy, and it makes her happy to make me happy. We have each made the decision to love the other, and when times are hard, we love each other more. When times are hard at home or at work, love the people around you more. Things will get better, or you'll learn it's time to leave.

Loving the people you work with doesn't make you weaker than them if they don't love you back. Loving a bad person makes you stronger than them because mature love requires you to see the person clearly and know who they are. Here's a story to show what I mean:

One brisk morning, a young boy was walking up a mountain when he saw a snake at the side of the trail. The snake said to the boy, "Boy! Pick me up and carry me down the mountain."

The boy said, "You're a snake. If I pick you up, you'll bite me."

The snake replied, "Please. I'm freezing. If you don't pick me up, I'll die."

So the boy picked up the snake and started to carry him down the mountain. After a little while, the snake said, "Boy, put me inside your coat," and the boy said, "If I put you inside my coat, you'll bite me, and I'll die."

"I won't bite you. I promise," the snake said. "I'm freezing. Please, put me inside your coat."

So the boy put the snake inside his coat. After a little while, the snake began to feel invigorated by the warmth of the boy, and his cold blood warmed again. The boy and the snake were almost to the end of the trail when the snake bit the boy. The boy dropped the snake, fell to one knee, and grabbed his chest where the snake had bitten him.

"Snake! You bit me, and now I'll die," the boy cried. "How could you do this to me?"

The snake said, "You knew I was a snake when you picked me up."

When we see snakes as snakes, we don't pick them up. We see them completely, so we protect ourselves when we love them.

Other People

How you come home from work is a great way to show the people you live with how you love them. When my kids were small, I often left work worn down and discouraged. Sometimes at dinner it was obvious I was feeling bad, so I started to play a game with my kids where I would make up stories about the animals that came to the office that day. If I felt run over, I might tell a story about angry rhinos. If I felt like something was blindingly stupid, I might tell a story about elephants who couldn't get through a door. Making my children laugh made the problem go away. I didn't have the confidence to find more rewarding employment, so instead I threw myself into being a good father who gave the kids baths, read them stories, and put them to bed. I remember the time when my children were small as a happy time, even though I was unhappy at work. I regret some of the time I spent in that job. I don't regret being present with my little kids. Having a dull job made that easier.

The next time you've had a hard day, take a moment in the driveway or at the front door and breathe. Collect yourself before you go in. Then go inside and look outside yourself for the light.

Your Organization

We demonstrate love by how we listen, how we act, and how we communicate, in rough order of importance. A great way to see how well your organization loves its customers is to give it a score—a Love Score. You can use the worksheet below to calculate a Love Score. 100 is tops, and 0 is nasty.

On the next page and to the right of each question, write how you score. Give yourself four points if you always do the action, three points if you usually do the action, two points if you sometimes do the action, and no points if you never do the action. If you score "Always" on every answer, give yourself a four-point bonus for a Love Score of 100.

TABLE 6: LOVE SCORE

SCORING: 4-ALWAYS, 3-USUALLY, 2-SOMETIMES, 0-NEVER	
The product works as promised	
Do we hear product complaints with an open mind and not assume "user error"?	SCORE
Do we prioritize getting existing features to work before adding new ones?	
Do we set good expectations about product performance and not overpromise?	
Customer feedback is sought, analyzed, and acted upon	
Do we schedule structured observations of customers?	
Are customer observations analyzed and shared widely?	
Do we update customers about what we're doing with their feedback?	
Customer support is responsive, proactive, empathic, and transparent	
Do we schedule feedback sessions?	
Do we acknowledge support issues immediately after we verify them?	
Do we proactively inform customers about their issues?	
Implementation and training are thorough and professional	
Do we allow customers to customize training and implementation?	
Are we organized with a time line and simple written plan?	
communicate progress and next steps?	

SCORING: 4-ALWAYS, 3-USUALLY, 2-SOMETIMES, 0-NEVER	
	SCORE
Do we listen for fears and concerns?	
Do we anticipate problems?	
Do we respond honestly to resistance to change?	
Product changes are communicated and supported	
Do we acknowledge defects?	
Can we roll back changes if we need to?	
Do we inform customers when changes are coming and explain changes after they happen?	
Disputes and conflicts are resolved responsibly and in the customer's interest	
Do we put aside our interests when listening to disputes?	
Do we offer reasonable compensation when a customer is unhappy?	
Do we acknowledge our mistakes without blaming?	
Customers feel valued and rewarded for loyalty	
Do customers have a forum on which to share successes?	
Do we thank customers with our actions?	
Do we acknowledge great customers publicly?	
TOTAL	

In business, love is self-interest rightly understood. Most commercial interactions are suboptimal—they stink or are unremarkable. Very few rise to the level of, "I loved that!" The ones that do achieve "I loved that!" win in the market. Customers become addicted to products they love. Addiction to a business enables that business to generate monopoly profits. As long as we keep feeling the love, we keep paying gladly.

Loving customers is hard work. Most organizations will score between 50 and 60. Work toward showing love in every communication, every action, every day, because giving love to customers is good for business. Let's not cheapen love when we talk about loving our customers. Let's really let it fly.

Chapter in a Chart: Make a Decision to Love Your Customers

Love looks like	⟶	Love doesn't look like
Seeing something or someone completely, warts and all.		Willfully ignoring what's wrong.
Listening before talking.		Talking without listening.
A fair exchange of value.		Giving everything away.
"If you lose this game, you'll take it to your [expletive] graves." —Herb Brooks, coach of the 1980 US Olympic hockey team, during the second intermission when the team was losing 2-1 in the gold medal game. The team went on to win 4-2.		"You guys are terrible!"
I once had to demonstrate my product for a competitive renewal to a customer who knew the product's every flaw. I put the best face I could on the software while being honest. We won because demos are never about the product; they're about the relationship.		I've been guilty of selling the future. It can be unavoidable in software. It's better to invite customers on a journey than to claim you've already arrived.

Why it matters	What to do about it
Love that only feels perfection and never pain isn't love; it's delusion.	Seek to know what's real. Don't overvalue yourself, your product, or your people, and don't undervalue them either. This is the work of a lifetime.
If you don't listen, you'll get trapped in your head, and there's more fantasy in your head than inspiration.	Remind yourself to ask someone how they are or what they're working on whenever you need something from them.
The more profit we generate, the more we can reinvest in our business and reward our employees, vendors, and investors.	Price based on perceived value. Create a lovable experience and charge a premium. If people love your product, they won't mind the premium.
Words make a difference. They can live forever. They can change the world. It's possible to inspire others with words. Don't be afraid to try.	Find the feeling, and the words will come. Even if the words don't come, if you project the feeling, people will know what you mean.
A sale based on a deception is a sin. It may build revenue, but it never builds value. You'll always carry the weight of the deception, even if your client never finds out, and that weight is a heavy burden.	Tell the truth in a way that puts your product in the best light, but don't deceive. I don't volunteer damaging information, which means I sometimes give incomplete answers, but I'm comfortable with it. You'll have to find that place for yourself.

Practice Step 3

Hint: "If you love everyone, even people you don't like, you will acquire power and be happy."

The scenario:

You're leading a critical integration project with a partner where the chief revenue officer (CRO) is the executive sponsor for the project. You held the project kickoff meeting with your team without the CRO because the CRO is too busy to come to any of your meetings.

Your junior developer looked at the partner's documentation, and says you're going to need to get one of the partner's developers on a meeting to know how to proceed. You wrote the CRO a note he can forward to everyone on the project where you identified your team members, their roles, and contact information. The CRO forwarded your note, with no changes, to his contact. She's a senior vice president (SVP) for partnerships.

You wrote another note to your CRO where you described your understanding of the project.

What should your call to action in your note to the CRO be?

If you want to write ...

⚙ "After making necessary edits, please send this project description to the following people (list the names of the people on the project) so we can proceed with the project," then go to page 63.

⚙ "Please respond confirming my understanding of the project," then go to page 65.

"AFTER MAKING NECESSARY EDITS, PLEASE SEND THIS PROJECT DESCRIPTION TO THE FOLLOWING PEOPLE (LIST THE NAMES OF THE PEOPLE ON THE PROJECT) SO WE CAN PROCEED WITH THE PROJECT."

The CRO made some tweaks to your description of the benefits of the project, then sent your note to the folks on your team and to his contact at the partner. A few minutes later, the SVP at the partner replied to the message, saying she's excited to be working with everyone and giving you the name of a technical contact at her company. You jumped on LinkedIn and saw that the contact is an IT project manager.

You sent the IT project manager at the partner a note to say your team is having trouble with their API documentation and asked if you can get someone with knowledge of their API to talk to your lead developer. A few days go by, and you get no response to your note.

If you want to …

- Draft a note to the partner for the CRO to send, then go to page 67.

- Send a note to the SVP at the partner, then go to page 69.

"PLEASE RESPOND CONFIRMING MY UNDERSTANDING OF THE PROJECT."

You send your note, but you don't hear anything back from the CRO. The next day you have a virtual check-in scheduled with your team, but no one shows up. You send a note to the lead developer, asking where they are, and get the response: "This project has no executive sponsor. I'm not wasting my time on it."

Yikes. How did this happen?

The project has a lot of things you can't control, like the executive sponsor's availability or the lead developer's attitude. You can make a decision to love everyone on the project, no matter how irritating they are. If you can love everyone, even when you don't like them and they don't love you, you will have more power than people who don't love you, because they won't be able to control you. You can't change the CRO, but you can see him for what he is and love him anyway. The CRO wants to feel in control but is too busy to be actively involved. He has no idea how to get the project done; that's why he needs you.

Love is a fair exchange of value, and the fair exchange here is that the CRO lets you borrow his prestige, and you use it to get the project done. Be more aggressive than asking for confirmation of your understanding, but do it in a way where you don't exceed your authority or make anyone look bad, particularly the CRO.

DRAFT A NOTE TO THE PARTNER FOR THE CRO TO SEND.

You write a note in the CRO's voice with the intention of having the CRO forward it directly to his SVP contact and the IT project manager who hasn't responded yet. The note says everyone at your company is ready to get going on the integration so you can move fast to market. You look on LinkedIn to find someone with a big title in the IT organization at your partner who might be a boss of the IT project manager who hasn't responded yet. You end your short note with "Is (name of IT project manager's boss) the right person to work with?"

The next day the CRO sends your note with some minor edits. About an hour later, you get an email from the IT project manager at the partner, suggesting a meeting between your teams. You respond, saying you need to discuss the documentation for their API and include a link to the documentation the junior developer found. A little while later, the IT project manager at the partner gets back to you with a link to a newer set of documentation. "We retired those other docs a year ago. Didn't know they were still out there. Thanks for finding them!"

You send the new documentation to the senior developer. He writes back, saying it has everything he needs to proceed.

Well done! The solution was simple, but the path was complicated because so many people and personalities were involved. You stepped up and acted like a leader without embarrassing anyone. Keeping your eye on the goal—getting the integration done—and not trying to control what you couldn't control—the CRO at your company and the SVP at the partner—was a great exercise in loving your customers. Plus, the implied threat of going to the boss of the IT project manager at the partner may not have hurt either.

Nice job.

SEND A NOTE TO THE SVP AT THE PARTNER.

A few days go by, and you hear nothing from the partner. You're about to forget the whole project when you get an email from your boss.

"CRO has asked me to take you off the partnership integration project. What gives?"

Yikes. How did this happen?

The CRO can't be actively involved, but you can't forget about him either. Sending a note directly to the SVP at the partner was too aggressive. You need to go through the CRO. He owns the relationship with the partner. Show your love by respecting that relationship.

Try hard to see people and accept them as they are; you don't have to like them. If you love them as they are, you won't try to make them change for you.

Go back to "Practice Step 3" on page 61 if you want to try again.

WHAT COMES NEXT

Before you can improve, you need an idea about what you want to become. The next chapter is about deciding what kind of person you want to be: a leader or an individual contributor. After you decide, you'll know more about how to focus your energy to spread the love.

Decide What Kind of Leader You Want to Be

There is nothing that can so justly spoil our taste for putting ourselves at pains for our leaders as to see those leaders meanwhile loafing about at paltry and frivolous occupations.
—MONTAIGNE

I command no one but myself, but I make my desires known.
—MARGARET THE PUG

Picasso changed the world without any direct reports. Margaret the pug gets most of what she wants despite not having hands or a voice. Whether we aspire to lead or not, we all create an example someone else might follow, so be the leader you want to follow. Don't loaf about at paltry occupations while others are working weekends.

Let's look back at our story of the interrupting salesperson to see how deciding what kind of leader you want to be plays out in life.

Imagine you're hard at work when a top-performing salesperson comes into your office. "You busy?" the salesperson asks. "I need to get a new feature into the next release. It's a big opportunity, and Biggie Cheese says we have to get this done."

"What's the opportunity?" you ask.

"This thing will make my year," the salesperson says. "And it's a takeaway from our biggest competitor. What they want us to do is super simple."

"Wow! That sounds awesome!"

"Yeah, this thing will either make my year or get me fired," says the salesperson. "I have a call with the prospect in five minutes."

"Mind if I sit in on the call?" you ask.

"I don't mind," says the salesperson, "as long as you don't talk about the product. It's the wrong time for that. If you want to say anything, write it down, and show me first."

Suppose you've decided that you're the sort of leader who stands up for what she believes, and you believe no one should be belittled at work. You push back and call the salesperson out for his "Write it down" comment. At best you still get to sit in the meeting with the prospect, but you'll upset the salesperson five minutes before an important call. Because the call is about closing a sale, other people in your organization are unlikely to take your side. A meeting with the prospect is too good an opportunity to let your ego get in the way, even if all you do is listen. You may hear the prospect's real needs as opposed to how those needs are presented by the salesperson. If you attend the call, you have a chance to clarify what's needed and build the salesperson's confidence. That's being a good person and a good leader. Be selfless: seek to understand before being understood, and drive toward the outcome you want. You want a

> Be selfless: seek to understand before being understood, and drive toward the outcome you want.

completed sale that doesn't commit the company to any promises. If the salesperson is anxious or nervous, they might put the company on the hook for something it can't deliver. People do crazy things under stress, and selling is stressful. If you respond as a parent, with love and guidance, you can help and learn.

You

The next time someone says something that makes you feel disrespected, ask yourself two questions before you respond:

1. Is this really about me?

2. Is this the right time to respond?

If the answer to either of those questions is "No," let it pass. If the answer to both is "Yes," then ask for what you deserve. In this case, the salesperson is five minutes away from perhaps the biggest deal of the year. His comment says more about him than about you.

Other People

Understanding your natural ambition will lead to a lot of freedom and peace of mind. If your heart's desire is to be a CEO, you'll be unhappy as anything else. Likewise, if you hate managing other people, you'll be more effective if you give it up.

If you decide you want to be a leader, you'll need to decide the scope of your leadership. Individual contributors lead by example. They master their craft, have a good work ethic, take direction well, and are curious and coachable. If you aren't a good individual contributor, you haven't earned the right to lead. Team leaders lead through influence rather than formal authority. Managers often refer to their direct reports as "my team." That's the wrong application of the word "team." Your team consists of your peers. The people who report to you are your responsibility; they're not your team. Eisenhower's team for the liberation of Europe was not the US Army. His team was the Allied commanders and political leaders who could strengthen the alliance. Managing a team isn't easy; you must influence and inspire. Be a team leader first.

Your Organization

Group leaders are responsible for a collection of teams, including everyone on those teams. Organization leaders are responsible for results achieved by the organization. Organization leaders are always operating with imperfect information, tweaking and adjusting to change results. Results are the product of many people's work, but the type of leader you are is your decision alone. Hold yourself accountable for what you can control: the type of person you are, good or bad. Think about your results too, but don't give yourself too much credit or blame. Results may be everything, but when assessing someone's character, including your own, they can be a distraction.

Chapter in a Chart: Decide What Kind of Leader You Want to Be

Good leaders ⟷ ▶	Bad leaders
Good leaders create conditions where others can do their best work and where the sum of that work creates something meaningful and valuable.	Bad leaders create conditions where others struggle to do good work and where the sum of the work is less than the individual pieces that constitute it.
Value character above competence	Confuse competence for character
Focus on pursuing the good	Overemphasize results
Keep their anxiety and irrationality to themselves	Spread their anxiety and irrationality to others
Make decisions	Avoid making decisions

Why it matters	What to do about it
There are more bad leaders than good leaders. Most people think about themselves too much.	Think about the kind of leader you want to follow and work to be that leader.
Results don't care about morals, but you should. Like Aristotle says, the payoff for virtue is eudaemonia (like "You dah Monia!"), which is usually translated as happiness, but it is more like a happiness that's worth dying for.	You can control your behavior, but you can't control your results. Being virtuous is completely within your control, and it guarantees a happy, fulfilling life, no matter the results of your work.
Athletes emphasize good fundamentals and following a good process. They know that results aren't up to them—a baseball player can hit the ball hard and still make an out.	The best you can do is influence the behavior of others. You can't control their behavior, but you don't have to tolerate it either. You can always send them packing or move on yourself.
I worked for a CEO who had a chronic health condition that caused him frequent pain. He never spoke about it. He knew it would be a distraction to others.	We all have anxiety and pain. You give up the right to share yours in public when you become a leader. Find a group of confidants you can share openly with and get whatever help you need.
A bad decision is often better than no decision. No decision creates a vacuum anything can fill.	Amazon really gets this right: make decisions fast if the decision can easily be reversed. Keep track of what happens. For decisions that are harder to change or irreversible, take your time, get as much input and data as you can, and then decide.

Practice Step 4

Hint: "You can decide what kind of leader to be, and you can decide not to be a leader at all."

The scenario:

You just finished a retrospective meeting with your team, and it didn't go well. The team missed its commitments for the third time in a row, and no one had a good explanation why. Besides missing commitments, you're taking heat for product defects, and your team ranks last in productivity metrics, which is unusual. You've been with your team for over a year, and they're usually high performers, if never good communicators.

You open your email. There's a message from the director of IT, the manager of the manager of the lead developer on your team. The subject is one word: "urgent."

"Invite me to all your meetings," the email says. "No exceptions."

How do you respond?

If you want to ...

- Reply to the director of IT and say it's a bad idea for him to come to all your meetings, go to page 83.

- Invite the director of IT to all your meetings, go to page 85.

REPLY TO THE DIRECTOR OF IT AND SAY IT'S A BAD IDEA FOR HIM TO COME TO ALL YOUR MEETINGS.

You write a note to the director of IT and explain as calmly as you can why it's a bad idea for him to attend all your meetings. You get no reply. A few days go by, and you get a note from your boss. The director of IT forwarded your note to him with one line—"FYI."

Your boss adds, "I'm taking you off the project. We'll talk about it when I get back next week. For now, don't do anything."

Yikes. Not an ideal outcome. How did this happen?

The director of IT is an excellent counterexample of a leader. If he got an email like the one you got, what would he probably do? He'd likely take it personally and make a fuss. That's what you did; you don't want to be that kind of leader. You don't know enough about the situation to say for sure that the director requested to be in your meetings because of something you did. Do what the director asked; invite him to all your meetings. It's very unlikely he'll actually come to all of them.

To try again, turn to page 81.

INVITE THE DIRECTOR OF IT TO ALL YOUR MEETINGS.

It takes a few minutes, and it's painful, but you invite the director of IT to all your meetings with the development team. You get a one-word email reply from the director: "Thanks."

A week goes by, and it's time for your next meeting with the team.

What should you do next? Read "Step 5: Make an Inventory of Your Character" to find out.

WHAT COMES NEXT

In the next chapter, you'll dig into your virtues and vices to understand who you are today and what you can become.

Make an Inventory of Your Character

To him who thinks none bad, whoever can seem good?
—MARTIAL, AS QUOTED BY MONTAIGNE

I never bury bones. I keep them all in my bed where I can find them.
—MARGARET THE PUG

An inventory is a counting of what you have in stock right now. Inventories are not about making judgments; they're about fact finding. Here's a story to show why taking a regular inventory of your character—your virtues and vices—matters.

You just finished a retrospective with your development team, and it didn't go well. The team missed its commitments for the third time in a row, and no one had a good explanation as to why. Besides missing commitments, you're taking heat for product defects, and your team ranks last in productivity metrics, which is unusual. You've been with your team for over a year, and they're usually high performers, if never good communicators.

You open your email. There's a message from the director of IT, the manager of the manager of the lead developer on your team. The subject is one word: "urgent."

"Invite me to all your meetings," the email says. "No exceptions."

If you have never taken an inventory, an email like this might ruin your day. If you take an inventory regularly, you'll be well prepared to respond because you'll understand your own character. What you need to know before you can respond well is "What is this email about?" Understanding your character, your virtues and vices, helps answer that.

You

Your character is not your abilities, such as intelligence or athleticism; it's your virtues and vices. We can't change our innate abilities. We can change our character because virtues and vices are about choice. According to Aristotle, a virtue is the mean between two extremes: one extreme is a deficiency of what's needed to meet a situation, the other extreme is an excess. The golden mean between two extremes is a virtue. For example, courage is the golden mean between rashness (not understanding danger) and cowardice (the inability to act in the face of danger). Any virtue taken to an extreme is a vice.

Let's think about the email you just got. Suppose you're a generous person. You share credit and want others to succeed. If your generosity sometimes causes you to sacrifice your well-being to support others, you might think the team's failures are all your fault, which is a kind of egotism. Anytime we think of ourselves like "I'm the best/worst" or "It's always/never about me," we're being egocentric. Egocentrism doesn't mean, "I love me more than anything"; that's narcissism. Egocentrism means your ego is the center of your life. When deciding how to respond to the email, don't put your ego at the center of your response.

Take a look at the list of virtues below. It's my own adaptation of virtues Aristotle describes in his *Nicomachean Ethics*. Put a √ in the column for anything that sings out, "This is me!"

TABLE 7: FIND YOUR VIRTUES

Virtue	What it means in practice	This is me!
Courage	After considering risks, you take actions and make decisions that can have a negative impact on you personally for the benefit of something larger than yourself.	
Moderation	You manage your desires and are not overoccupied with pleasure or distraction.	
Generosity	You share money wisely, giving the right amount to the right people at the right time, without regard for getting credit or creating advantage for yourself.	
Gentleness	You're slow to anger, and when you get angry, it's for the right reasons and directed at the right people in the right way.	
Friendliness	You don't cause others pain by being rude or selfish, you don't flatter, and you don't debase yourself to anyone.	
Truthfulness	You clearly understand your qualities. You don't boast or talk yourself down.	
Wittiness	You're charming and a good conversationalist. You're funny without acting like a fool. You're not dull or a buffoon.	
Right ambition	You have a desire to earn honors for the right reasons. You want to be recognized for excellence but not at the expense of your character.	

If you're honest with yourself and you're less than eighty years old, you won't have all these virtues yet. That's OK. Any one of these virtues can be the foundation for an empire. Jerry Seinfeld has a billion-dollar career founded on being witty. He's many other things, but if he wasn't witty, none of them would matter much. Washington was a courageous person, but his superpower was that he was truthful. He didn't boast despite being adored. If you're moderate and have the right ambition, you probably won't take the email about inviting the supervisor to every meeting personally. Your pride might be hurt, but you'll see past that to the bigger issue: fixing the team's performance. That's the right ambition here; fix the team.

Now suppose you're courageous. You love your team and know having their boss in every meeting will kill their morale. You send a note back, saying it's a terrible idea for the boss to be in every meeting. What might happen? Anybody who sends a note that says, "Invite me to all your meetings, no exceptions," is too paranoid or too selfish to understand your courage. You need to check your courage before you respond. Suppose sometimes you don't have as much ambition as you should. Maybe you don't care so much that the team is doing poorly. That's not good. If you've been given a position of leadership, you're responsible for performance. You have nothing to gain and a lot to lose by shirking your responsibility. What if you're too moderate at work? You might carry a lot of tension around. A note like "Invite me to all your meetings" could give you a neck ache for a week. Even moderate people need to feel emotion. Anger and annoyance are good reactions to this note, but you can't stay angry and annoyed if you want to fix the team and improve your relationship with the supervisor who wrote the note.

Vices are raw material for virtues. Bill Gates created a near monopoly and became rich. His oversized ambition and lack of generosity were critical assets in the creation of that near monopoly. Mr. Gates still wants to do great things, but the things he does are for humanity's benefit; he rightsized his ambition and generosity until they became virtues. So don't try to fix your vices just now; just name them. This is an inventory, or a diagnosis, if you prefer. If you go to the doctor, and she takes an X-ray and sees you have a broken foot, that doesn't mean you're broken. It might even be good news. "Oh! Now I know why it hurts when I walk! I thought I had bone cancer!" It's the same with your character. Character can be managed and improved, but only if you look at it. Your character inventory is not a judgment about being good or bad; it's a chance to know what's real so you can begin to manage it and make it better.

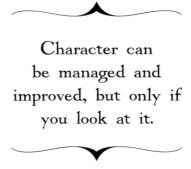

Character can be managed and improved, but only if you look at it.

Take a look at the following list. Don't be scared; this is an inventory, not a grade. It's just a point-in-time thing. Character is always changing, just like the stock in a warehouse is always changing. Sometimes we run out of courage or wittiness and need to order a little more. If we don't make an accurate count, we'll never know. So make an honest count. Circle the phrase or phrases in each row that best describe you. When you're done, each row should have either one or two phrases circled.

TABLE 8: YOUR SELF-DIAGNOSIS

I'm sometimes like this	I'm always like this	I'm sometimes like this
You're fearful, lack confidence and spirit, or you're unable to make difficult decisions.	After considering risks, you take actions and make decisions that can have a negative impact on you personally for the benefit of something larger than yourself.	You take stupid risks or overindulge in dangerous activities.
You're over the top or out of control.	You manage your desires and are not overoccupied with pleasure or distraction.	You're unable to take pleasure from things.
You're selfish and fearful with money.	You share money wisely, giving the right amount to the right people at the right time, without regard for getting credit or creating advantage for yourself.	You're thoughtless and overly casual with money.
You're irritable, touchy, easily bothered, or you can't take a joke.	You're slow to anger, and when you get angry, it's for the right reasons and directed at the right people in the right way.	You won't defend yourself.
You're rude or thoughtless.	You don't cause others pain by being rude or selfish, you don't flatter, and you don't debase yourself to anyone.	You flatter, manipulate, or fake interest.
You fake humility or talk yourself down.	You clearly understand your qualities. You don't boast or talk yourself down.	You exaggerate your qualities; you bullshit about things you know little about.
You're dull or can't make a joke.	You're charming and a good conversationalist. You're funny without acting like a fool. You're not dull or a buffoon.	You can't help but make a joke of everything.
You have little drive or don't care about quality.	You have a desire to earn honors for the right reasons. You want to be recognized for excellence but not at the expense of your character.	You're a glory hound or a praise pig.

You might be thinking, "This chart isn't fair. No one is ever 'always' anything." Exactly right, and that's the point. We can always improve our character. The goal isn't to be friendly or moderate or witty often; it's to always be friendly, moderate, or witty, and we all fall short, but that's the goal. All your vices can become virtues if you moderate them. It's like counting calories; counting your calories is the best way to lose weight. I don't have to judge my calories; I just have to count them. It's the same with my vices. If I can name my vices (e.g., "I don't stick up for myself"), and take a daily inventory to monitor them, I can manage them until they become virtues. Don't get impatient. If you're fortunate, your life will be long.

Other People

Knowing your virtues and vices—your character—helps you understand why some of your work relationships are difficult. What you consider to be a virtue might be seen as a vice by a colleague. If you're happy being an individual contributor, what other people think of your character doesn't matter; just be excellent at your job. If you aspire to lead, what other people think means a lot. If you think you're a moderate person, someone else might think you lack passion or commitment. If you're a gentle person, you might take too much blame for a team's performance. That won't help you professionally, and it won't make the team better. You need to investigate before

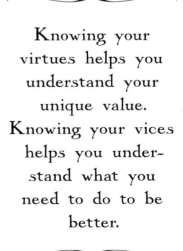

Knowing your virtues helps you understand your unique value. Knowing your vices helps you understand what you need to do to be better.

assuming the poor performance is because of you. Knowing your virtues helps you understand your unique value. Knowing your vices helps you understand what you need to do to be better.

Your Organization

Gentleness is a great virtue for grammar school teachers but not combat leaders. Is your character suitable for your organization? Organizational culture is like gravity: we can't see or define it, but we sure can feel it. It's possible for your work to consistently exceed the limits of your organization's culture in the same way flying to the moon is possible; it takes a ton of energy and a lot of personal risk. If you aren't comfortable in your organization's culture, you'll need the energy of a rocket to burst through and escape it. Rockets don't carry many people. Your small team may be able to find a comfortable orbit, but you'll never carry the whole organization with you. The more aligned your character is with the character of your organization, the less it will cost you personally to accumulate power and lead.

Chapter in a Chart: Make an Inventory of Your Character

Virtue looks like ⟹	Leadership looks like
Loving others exactly as they are, even if we hate what they do. Love the sinner, hate the sin.	Never playing favorites.
Living for ideas and for others.	Accumulating and exercising power, for good or ill.
Pardoning offenses.	Serving justice.
Acknowledging when your product falls short of its promise.	Acknowledging shortfalls publicly to a customer.
Confidence in the face of hardship.	Inspiring confidence in others.
The Saint Francis prayer. Turn to page 290 if you are unfamiliar with this prayer.	The Saint Francis prayer.

Why it matters	➡	What to do about it
We can only get so good at loving the people we like. The master class is loving the humanity in people we hate.		Most of us think about ourselves too much to see others clearly. Think more about others, and you'll discover yourself.
Aristotle says that to have meaningful and lasting happiness, we have to be virtuous. Leadership has nothing to do with happiness. Leadership is about power.		Don't become a leader to make yourself happy. Become a leader to serve others—which will make you happy—and to accumulate power.
Even self-effacing leaders who put the interests of others before themselves need to exercise power.		Use the power you have to make other lives better. Don't hoard power just to have it. Power not used is power wasted.
Virtue is table stakes. Customers want us to be leaders.		Take responsibility and define the path to a better outcome. Admit faults, but never dwell on them. Focus on the future.
Somebody has to pick the team up when it's down. Anybody who can be honest while being hopeful can do it.		Shine your love on the people around you. Compliment them honestly. Show them you love them by how you look at them.
There's a lot of "I" and "me" in the Saint Francis prayer. That's because it's a prayer for accumulating power: the power to help others, to influence them, to bring peace and hope where confusion was before.		If you want to accumulate a lot of power, learn to do everything in the St. Francis prayer: "Where there is discord, let me bring union/Where there is error, let me bring truth." Bringing union and truth; that's power, baby.

Practice Step 5

Hint: "You can change your character, and a good character leads to a good life."

The scenario:

Your team is missing commitments and is struggling with productivity. You've been with your team for over a year, and they're usually high performers, if never good communicators.

You got an email from the director of IT, the manager of the manager of the lead developer on your team. The subject is one word: "urgent."

"Invite me to all your meetings," the email says. "No exceptions."

It takes a few minutes, and it's painful, but you invite the director of IT to all your meetings with the development team. You get a one-word email reply from the director: "Thanks."

A week goes by, and it's time for your next meeting with the team.

What should you do next?

If you want to …

⚙ Lead the meeting with the team as usual, go to page 103.

⚙ Ask your boss if he can come to the meeting too, go to page 105.

LEAD THE MEETING WITH THE TEAM AS USUAL.

The director of IT comes, although he's on his phone the whole meeting. The lead developer asks more questions than usual, although the team seems a little surprised by some of the questions. You feel like the lead developer doesn't know this section of the code as well as he should.

Overall, the meeting goes well, and you're able to end a few minutes early.

"Do you have a few minutes to talk?" you ask.

The director nods and takes a seat. "I hear you have a problem with my team," he says.

"The team is fine," you say. "I have a problem with our performance."

The director smiles. "I do too. What do you think the problem is?"

"It feels like something is going on that I'm not aware of," you say.

The director leans back and sighs. "There is something, but I can't really talk about it. The team is floundering with technical issues that shouldn't take so much time. After code review, they're having to rewrite a lot of code to bring it up to spec. That shouldn't be happening, but we're working on it. I just need everyone to be patient."

How should you respond?

If you want to say …

⚙ "Having you in the meetings will only put more pressure on the team," go to page 82.

⚙ "What are you looking for by coming to these meetings?" go to page 79.

ASK YOUR BOSS IF HE CAN COME TO THE MEETING TOO.

You send a note to your boss and ask if he can come to the team meeting. He responds with a note: "When I ask for leadership, this isn't what I mean. It's not a good idea for me to be there."

What should you do?

If you want to ...

⊛ Lead the meeting with the team as usual, go to page 103.

⊛ Tell the director of IT "Having you in the meetings will only put more pressure on the team," then go to page 111.

"WHAT ARE YOU LOOKING FOR BY COMING TO THESE MEETINGS?"

"I'm looking at the dynamics. You have some very talented people on that team. They should be crushing it. That's why I think there's a leadership problem. Your lead developer was my first hire. He's been around longer than just about anybody here. And your junior developer would be the senior on any other team." He pauses a moment and continues. "You guys are last in productivity, you know."

How should you respond?

If you want to say ...

- ⚙ "Having you in the meetings will only put more pressure on the team," go to page 111.

- ⚙ "We can move the lead dev to defects. He knows that code better than anyone. The junior dev gets to act as senior dev. You said he'd be a senior on any other team," go to page 109.

"WE CAN MOVE THE LEAD DEV TO DEFECTS. HE KNOWS THAT CODE BETTER THAN ANYONE. THE JUNIOR DEV GETS TO ACT AS SENIOR DEV. YOU SAID HE'D BE A SENIOR ON ANY OTHER TEAM."

"You'd be down a senior developer," says the director. "It would kill your productivity."

"We're already last in productivity. It's worth a try. At least we'll make progress on defects," you answer.

The director chuckles. "What harm can it do, right? OK, we'll move your senior dev to defects and give your junior dev a battlefield promotion. The project can continue, and we'll address defects. But if product chews us out for being late, I'm going to say it was your idea."

"Sounds like a plan," you say.

The director is as good as his word and moves your senior developer onto defects later that day. You meet with the junior developer right after the announcement. He's concerned about the lead developer, but he's also relieved and excited about the opportunity.

You have a planning meeting the next day to talk about how the team will adjust to the loss of the senior developer. No one seems concerned about lost productivity. The next few weeks feel like a weight has been lifted. You hit all your commitments and begin working ahead. The junior developer is a star. He knows the new code and is loved by the team. Despite being smaller than every other team, you're second in productivity.

Even the old lead developer is happier. He's knocking out defects and training the rest of the developers on the old code.

In six months, the new features are released on time, sales are up, and the organization has a new director of IT.

Success! Well done!

"HAVING YOU IN THE MEETINGS WILL ONLY PUT MORE PRESSURE ON THE TEAM."

The director frowns. "My people love me. Anytime one of them is feeling threatened, I'm going to stick up for them. I'm going to ask your boss to take you off the project."

Not the ideal outcome. What went wrong?

You can't control that the director of IT is paranoid. You're better off accepting that. You can improve the dynamics of your team. Your internal customers—your development team—are suffering. They keep missing deadlines, have quality problems, and are under a lot of pressure. Even if he's paranoid, the IT director is the best path to make things better for your team; you have to talk with him. You have to have a conversation with the director of IT. He can't come to all your meetings, but he can help with your team's dynamics. When you talk to the director of IT, make the conversation about performance and helping customers. Everyone around you is super touchy. You can't afford to take anything personally.

Turn to page 101 to try again.

WHAT COMES NEXT

In the next chapter, you'll think of stories from your life that demonstrate the virtues and vices you identified in this chapter. Then you'll share those stories with a trusted friend to see if you're being a good judge of your own character.

Share Your Inventory with a Trusted Friend

No hiding place rewards the wicked ... since their
conscience exposes them to themselves.
—EPICURUS AS QUOTED BY MONTAIGNE

Even those of us who don't talk need someone to listen to them.
—MARGARET THE PUG

Every Saturday I talk with a friend I've known for twenty years. We discuss our weeks, what we're reading, what we're watching on TV, baseball, and everything else on our minds. After I tell my friend what's weighing on me, what I feel guilty about, what I wish I had done better, I feel better. We talk and listen and help each other live better lives. Getting better at something requires practice and helpful feedback, even if the something you're getting better at is living. When you tell another person your story, you get perspective you can't get from looking in the mirror. Even if you don't have a close friend you can share your vulnerabilities with, you can learn by reading things by people you admire and by meditating. It's harder but not impossible to improve your character without a close friend. You'll have to be especially honest with yourself since you'll have no one to be honest for you.

Honesty is not an excuse to be rude to yourself or anyone else. If you want to get the most from sharing your inventory with a trusted friend, you need to pick the right time and place. Here's an example of why timing is important:

You were about to leave the office to meet your partner to celebrate their birthday over dinner when you got an urgent request from your boss. Your boss is meeting with the CEO tomorrow and needs a report from you to prepare. The report is going to take five or six hours to put together. You don't want to skip dinner because things have been tough between you and your partner lately, and you're hoping this dinner gets you back on track. You arrive at the restaurant. Your partner can see you're a bit distracted. What should you do?

If you tell your partner, "I have to write a report for my boss," you'll make dinner about you. That's not fair; it's your partner's birthday, and they've chosen to spend the one birthday they have a year with you. Tell your partner about the report after you've enjoyed dinner together; apologize that you have to leave, and go pull an all-nighter if you have to. That's how you show love for your partner and your boss.

You

When you were faced with a situation that required courage or moderation or wittiness, how did you react? Think about stories from your life. You can use the form on the next few pages as a template.

TABLE 9: VIRTUE IN PRACTICE: BLANK FORM

Virtue	What it means in practice
Courage	After considering risks, you take actions and make decisions that can have a negative impact on you personally for the benefit of something larger than yourself.

When I got this right

When I missed

Virtue	What it means in practice
Moderation	You manage your desires and are not overoccupied with pleasure or distraction.

When I got this right

When I missed

Generosity	You share valuable things wisely, giving the right amount to the right people at the right time, without regard for getting credit or creating advantage for yourself.

When I got this right

When I missed

Gentleness	You are slow to anger, and when you get angry, it's for the right reasons and directed at the right people in the right way.

When I got this right

When I missed

Friendliness	You don't cause others pain by being rude or selfish, you don't flatter, and you don't debase yourself to anyone.

When I got this right

When I missed

Truthfulness	You clearly understand your qualities. You don't boast or talk yourself down.

When I got this right

When I missed

| **Wittiness** | You're charming and a good conversationalist. You're funny without acting like a fool. You're not dull or a buffoon. |

When I got this right

When I missed

| **Right ambition** | You have a desire to earn honors for the right reasons. You want to be recognized for excellence but not at the expense of your character. |

When I got this right

When I missed

I've filled out each box with my own personal examples to give
you ideas.

TABLE 9: VIRTUE IN PRACTICE: BLANK FORM

Virtue	What it means in practice
Courage	After considering risks, you take actions and make decisions that can have a negative impact on you personally for the benefit of something larger than yourself.

When I got this right: I asked my wife to marry me when I was twenty-three and she was thirty-one. People told me I was too young. I saw friends breaking up not because they didn't love each other but because they were scared. I wasn't scared. Our relationship is bigger than me.

When I missed: I wanted to write screenplays when I got out of college. We were living in Nashville. There were no screenwriting jobs in Nashville. I never asked Anna to go to California so I could be a screenwriter. I sold us both short.

Moderation	You manage your desires and are not overoccupied with pleasure or distraction.

When I got this right: I don't drink anymore because I don't take the first drink. By not taking one drink a day—the first one—I stay sober.

When I missed: I never just eat the ice cream in my bowl. After I finish what's in my bowl, I always eat more from the carton before I put it away. I'm about ten pounds overweight, and I feel guilty about it, but I'm not trying to change.

Generosity	You share valuable things wisely, giving the right amount to the right people at the right time, without regard for getting credit or creating advantage for yourself.

When I got this right: When someone I'm responsible for does something well, I praise them in public if I can, and I always praise them in private.

When I missed: Sometimes I've been slow to hire people when I can do something myself. This has held the growth of my business back.

Gentleness	You are slow to anger, and when you get angry, it's for the right reasons and directed at the right people in the right way.

When I got this right: People who have reported to me who did great work have left me for another job, sometimes even after saying they wouldn't. I'm always sad for myself, but I still manage to celebrate their victory.

When I missed: My daughter broke the glass aquarium we kept her gerbil in after I told her to be careful. She was nine, and I got angrier than I'd ever been with her, which means I yelled so loud I scared her. Stupid.

Friendliness	You don't cause others pain by being rude or selfish, you don't flatter, and you don't debase yourself to anyone.

When I got this right: I try to learn something about the people I'm with, even if we're just in line for food at the office holiday party.

When I missed: My old CEO would think out loud. I used to think with him, talking about all the work we'd have to do to accomplish what he was talking about. I thought I was being helpful. He heard it as being negative. Later I learned to roll with what he said rather than resist it.

Truthfulness	You clearly understand your qualities. You don't boast or talk yourself down.

When I got this right: I know I'm a good listener. I put this to work as the host of a webinar business that created over a million dollars in value and never lost money.

When I missed: When I was younger, I wouldn't have written, "as the host of a webinar business that created over a million dollars in value," because it sounds boastful, but it really happened, and I'm proud of it. False modesty isn't a virtue.

Wittiness	You're charming and a good conversationalist. You're funny without acting like a fool. You're not dull or a buffoon.

When I got this right: When I was in my early thirties, I had to eat a lot of meals with customers who were older than my parents. I asked questions and listened a lot. When they asked about me, I never shrank from talking about being a young father.

When I missed: Early in our marriage, I applied for a job as a waiter at a fancy restaurant. The manager asked, "Why do you want to work here?" I said, "Because I need the money." I didn't get the job.

Right ambition	You have a desire to earn honors for the right reasons. You want to be recognized for excellence but not at the expense of your character.

When I got this right: I wrote this book despite all the times I've thought, "Who cares what I think?" I care. That's enough.

When I missed: I waited five years longer than I should have to get out of a job where I wasn't growing. Things have turned out well, but I still regret it.

If you find the chart hard to fill out, try going down the columns and writing all your "When I got this right" entries before writing your "When I missed." You don't need to fill out every box. Just do the ones that come easily.

Other People

Who you share your list with is important. Tell people you're taking an inventory of your character so you can develop your virtues and minimize your vices. People who care about you will want to help. It's best to share your entire list with one person, but you don't have to share it with only one person. You can break your list up and ask several people about one or two items on it to confirm what you learned when you shared the whole list with one person. The people you share your list with don't have to have the same job you do, but it helps if they have familiarity with your work. When you begin, let them know you're looking for real feedback about what you do well and what you're not so good at. The purpose of the conversation is to assess your virtues honestly so you can build on them while moderating your vices. Remember your list is about your character, not your skills. When you share your list, don't be defensive. Don't respond right away to comments that sound like criticism. In fact, a good habit is not to respond at all to anything that sounds like criticism. Sleep on it for a night. If you're still sore the next day, ask yourself if it's because the critique dug up something real you need to deal with or because you're annoyed by a false accusation. If it's the latter, let it go. Maybe you just chose the wrong person to share your list with. If it's the former, and you're sore because you have an issue to deal with, be grateful for the pain. It's likely a much smaller pain you feel from the observation of a friend than you would feel if the vice was pointed out because of a public blowup.

Your Organization

You probably don't want to share your list of virtues with your supervisor. Most supervisors want happy, hardworking people who bring them solutions, not problems. Bringing a list of virtues and vices to your supervisor sounds like you're asking them to do work for you.

Your family and friends are an organization too.

You may want to share an abbreviated list after you've fully shared with someone other than your supervisor to show you're developing the habit of self-assessment, but if you have a supervisor who's always on the sniff for weakness, probably not.

Your family and friends are an organization too. You may display similar behaviors in your personal life as you do in your work life. If you are obsessive about planning at work, you're likely obsessive at home too. Understanding how your obsessiveness affects others can benefit you both at home and work. You need to know how your habits affect others, both positively and negatively. One of the perks of leadership is you can make people work around your habits, so you can choose to ignore how your habits negatively affect others. Just know that if you do that, good people will leave you.

Chapter in a Chart: Share Your Inventory with a Trusted Friend

When you share your story ➡	When you hold back
You find out what you're good at.	You get stuck in your head without a clear sense of what's important.
You're vulnerable because you share specifics and details.	You don't learn anything because you only talk in generalities.
You own your part.	You blame others or pretend nothing is wrong.
You find you're not as good at some things as you thought.	You don't get a true picture of your value.
You find the work that comes easily to you is often the most valuable work you do.	You don't listen or believe people when they compliment or criticize you. You undervalue or overvalue your work.

Why it matters	What to do about it
Your character is your unique blend of virtues and vices.	Look at your résumé. Think about how you've been able to accomplish what you've done. That's your character.
You may find the person you are sharing with has similar stories and already knows how your story is going to turn out.	You can share more frankly and get better feedback from people who don't work in the same organization you work in. Make sure you're cultivating professional relationships with people you admire outside your organization.
I've had to deliver a lot of bad news to customers. I never make a joke of it. I explain as simply as I can what happened, take responsibility, and move to something positive.	Be honest and don't dramatize. A wonderful phrase to use when you hear criticism or suggestions you don't agree with is "You might be right." Let the suggestion simmer awhile before acting on it or throwing it out.
You have to understand your true value to get the most value from your life.	Watch your vices, but don't obsess about them. Obsess about your virtues.
Sharing your stories with someone you trust helps confirm what you do well.	Do more of what you're good at. Seek honest feedback about it. Believe what the people who love you say. Put in the work to get better.

Practice Step 6

Hint: "You need other people to learn what will make you happy."

The scenario:

You have a dinner date scheduled with your romantic partner for their birthday. It's at a hot new restaurant that's difficult to get reservations to. The two of you have been stressed out and not communicating lately. You've both been looking forward to dinner all week so you can get back on track. You're about to leave the office a little early when you receive an email from your boss. The subject is "Need this by 9 tomorrow."

It's a request for a report she wants to share with the CEO. You have to collect and summarize a lot of data from many different sources because she's making a pitch to invest in your group. Her meeting got moved up a week because the CEO has to travel unexpectedly.

You don't have a template, but you've talked with your boss about the report, and you have a good idea what she wants. It could be five or six hours of work.

While driving home you call your boss. She picks up.

"Do you mind if I sit in on your meeting with the CEO tomorrow? I'll have the report done, but it won't be as polished as I like because it's my partner's birthday tonight, and we have reservations at Chateau Hard-to-Get-Into."

"Sounds good. Let's meet tomorrow at 9, and you can walk me through it," your boss says.

You get home, change your clothes, pick up your gift, and get to the restaurant a few minutes early. Your partner comes in the door and looks great.

"Hello, beautiful," your partner
says. "How was your day?"

If you want to respond ...

⊛ "Awesome, now that I'm here with you," go to page 133.

⊛ "You don't want to know," go to page 135.

"AWESOME, NOW THAT I'M HERE WITH YOU."

Your partner smiles and takes your hand. You're shown to your table. The restaurant has a happy buzz. You're excited to be out, but in the back of your mind, you're thinking about the meeting tomorrow.

After the drinks arrive, your partner says, "You seem a little distracted. Everything OK?"

If you want to respond ...

- ⊛ "I have a meeting with the CEO tomorrow," go to page 137.
- ⊛ "Things are good. What was your best birthday as a kid?" go to page 139.

"YOU DON'T WANT TO KNOW."

"Oh, boy. Here we go again. What is it now?"

"I have a meeting tomorrow with the CEO."

"Well, good for you. You know tonight's my birthday? But I suppose you need to cut out early. Why didn't you tell me before now? I could have come with someone who wants to be here."

After the drinks arrive, your partner says, "Let's just forget it. You go back to work. I'm going to the bar," and gets up from the table and leaves.

Yikes. How did this happen?

Tonight is your partner's night. If you want to be a good partner, think about how you would want to be treated in the same situation. You probably wouldn't want your partner to make the conversation about them and their job. Decide what kind of partner you want to be, and think about when things went well with your partner. If you can, be that person.

Go back to "Practice Step 6" on page 129 if you want to try again.

"I HAVE A MEETING TOMORROW WITH THE CEO."

"I suppose you need to cut out early," your partner says. "Why didn't you tell me before now? I could have come with someone who wants to be here. Let's just forget it. You go back to work. I'm going to the bar," and walks away.

Yikes. How did this happen?

Tonight is your partner's night. If you want to be a good partner, think about how you would want to be treated in the same situation. You probably wouldn't want your partner to make the conversation about them and their job. Think about Step 4, decide what kind of partner you want to be, and take a little inventory on how you can show you love better.

Go back to "Practice Step 6" on page 129 if you want to try again.

"THINGS ARE GOOD. WHAT WAS YOUR BEST BIRTHDAY AS A KID?"

Your partner leans back and smiles. "Oh, that has to be my sixteenth birthday." Your partner goes into a long, funny story, and you're reminded why you liked your partner in the first place. You spend dinner telling each other funny stories about good and bad birthdays and holidays. It's good to feel the old warmth and know you haven't heard all their stories yet.

Dinner is delicious, but the best part is sitting across from each other. After dessert you go into the parking lot. Your partner takes your hand and says, "Follow me home?"

"I can't. I have a meeting with the CEO tomorrow I need to prepare for."

"Oh my god, why didn't you tell me?"

"I didn't want to spoil dinner," you say. "It's a really good opportunity. I'm just sorry it happened today."

"That's so thoughtful," your partner says. "Tell you what. I'll go home, get in my pajamas, and wait. Send me a text when you finish."

"It will probably be tomorrow. Can you stay in your pajamas that long?"

"Oh, you know I can." You kiss goodnight and go back to your car. Your heart is beating so much you won't need coffee to make it through this all-nighter.

You go back to your place to prepare the reports. You make a bulleted list of data that supports all your projections and your budget. You also create one graph that shows your revenue, expense, and profit projections, as well as a list of potential risks and mitigations. It's not as much as you would do if you had more time to prepare, but it's enough to demonstrate your thinking. You get to bed around four.

You're back at the office in enough time to get everything together for your 9:00 a.m. with your boss. You and your boss spend a few hours tweaking the graph and polishing the list of risks and mitigations. She also asks you to create a list of all your sources so the CEO can see you did your homework.

"This is great, thanks. I don't think you need to come to the meeting," your boss says.

If you want to respond ...

⊛ "Sounds good," go to page 143.

⊛ "What if he asks about one of the sources? You haven't had time to read them all yet," go to page 145.

"SOUNDS GOOD."

The next day you see your boss after her meeting with the CEO. "How did it go?" you ask.

"Not so good. We looked unprepared. He asked about one of your sources, and I had no idea what to say. I believe his exact words were, 'Looks like you haven't finished your homework.'" You can tell by her expression that she blames you.

Yikes. How did this happen?

Sometimes love means telling someone something they need to hear rather than what they want to hear. In this case, your boss needed to hear that taking the meeting without you was riskier than taking it with you. The plan was your work. You needed to be in the meeting with the CEO in case any questions came up that your boss couldn't answer.

Think about the type of leader you want to be. If you want to be the sort of leader who shares credit and allows others to be in meetings with the CEO, you can show that sort of leadership by giving your boss the opportunity to be that kind of leader. Even if you don't care about face time with the CEO, you're letting your boss down by letting her go into the meeting alone.

Go back to page "Practice Step 6" on page 129 if you want to try again.

"WHAT IF HE ASKS ABOUT ONE OF THE SOURCES? YOU HAVEN'T HAD TIME TO READ THEM ALL YET."

"That is just the kind of thing he'd do," your boss says. "You'd better come. You don't need to say anything unless there's something I can't answer."

You go to the meeting with your boss, and sure enough, the CEO asks about one of the sources your boss hasn't read. You're able to answer his question to show you've done the work required to back up your recommendations.

"Looks like you two did your homework," the CEO says.

"He's a great helper," your boss says, referring to you.

"Helper, huh?" the CEO says. "I imagine you did most of this work," the CEO says, pointing at you. "Otherwise, why would you be here?"

Your boss looks like a caught rabbit.

"Sounds like more than a helper to me," the CEO says.

Your budget is approved. You have another meeting with the CEO a month later, this time by yourself. He tells you how impressed he was with your work and says he's spinning off a small group from your boss's group, "So it can get the leadership it deserves. I want you to lead it."

Well done! You honored your commitments, made your partner happy, and got a promotion, all because you took ownership of your commitments and didn't ask anyone else to adjust for you. You did the work, and you got the rewards.

WHAT COMES NEXT

Now that you've made your list and shared it with a friend, it's time to develop your character. In the next chapter, you'll learn how to do that.

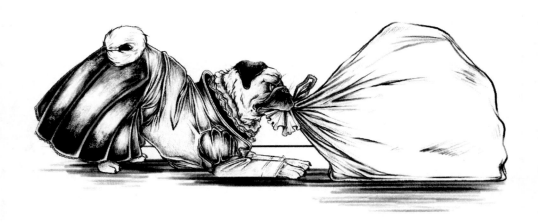

Embrace Your Character—All of It

He who follows another follows nothing. He finds
nothing; indeed he seeks nothing. 'We are not under
a king; let each one claim his own freedom.'
—SENECA AS QUOTED BY MONTAIGNE

I'll never drag a dead bird out of a lake, but I still have my charms.
—MARGARET THE PUG

Performance is shaped by character. With my best swing, I can drive a golf ball 270 yards; that's my ability. My ability naturally grows until I reach maturity, and then it declines with age. I can't change my natural ability, but I can use my character to develop it. (If I had the right ambition, I'd lift weights to hit the ball farther, but I don't.) Performance is how well I hit the ball, and outcomes are what happens after I hit the ball. If there's a twenty-mile-an-hour wind at my back, the ball might go 290 yards if I hit it on the screws. I didn't suddenly acquire more ability then; I just got lucky. I need to develop my character to get the most from my ability. I develop my character by nurturing my virtues and moderating my vices. You can't get the

149

most out of your character or your abilities if you overvalue your virtues or despise your vices. Virtues can change into vices; vices are just unmoderated virtues. You need to embrace your whole character to master it.[5]

David Ortiz was one of the best hitters in professional baseball during his time with the Boston Red Sox. He was also one of the worst players when it came to catching and throwing the ball. The Red Sox recognized that David was very good at offense and terrible at defense. Instead of working endlessly to get better at defense, where David never would have been better than very bad no matter how hard he worked, the Red Sox made David their designated hitter, a position that doesn't play defense. It's also a position that rarely wins awards because it's not respected. The Red Sox and David both showed character—courage, generosity, gentleness, and right ambition—when they made David a designated hitter. During David's fourteen years with the Red Sox, the team won three World Series titles, and David was an All-Star ten times. That's a lot of success for a player who's terrible at half of what a baseball player does. It shows the power of using character to focus on what you're good at and having the courage to live with the rest.

You

Embracing your whole character is hard when you're at the start of your career. For one thing, you don't have enough experience to understand your virtues and vices. For another, you don't get to pick the work you do; it's assigned to you. So how can you develop your virtues and moderate your vices when you don't control the work assigned to you? By exercising your character. A lot of work is drudgery.

---

5   "Life is neither good nor evil in itself: it is the scene of good or evil according as you give them room." — Montaigne

Even Tim Cook has to go to meetings he'd rather skip. Work is work. Like Montaigne says, "Practice at enduring work is practice at enduring pain." If you use work as a way to shape your character, your work will have more meaning. I've only had to dig one dry well in my life. I did it with two other guys, and I didn't mind it too much because I was lonely, and digging the well gave me an outlet. I dug a friendly well. How you perform your work says more about you than it does about the work. I worked in a kitchen before I was married. I was slow, too slow to

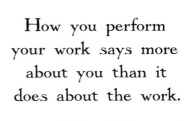

How you perform your work says more about you than it does about the work.

work in a really busy kitchen, but I always showed up, and I cared about the food. You can always do the same thing no matter how crummy your job is. Don't fight the part of you that hates your work; that part is trying to tell you something. Think hard about why you hate your work—is it because you're bad at it? Is it because of the people you work with? Is it because it bores you? After you find out why you hate your work, take appropriate action. Moderate what keeps you from being present, or amplify what tells you to do something else. If you can't care about the food, get out of the kitchen.

Other People

Vices are like enormous boomerangs; they come back to us eventually, but it can take decades. In the meantime, you might be having a party, but the people around you are miserable. You might have more courage or moderation than the people you work with. Embrace it, but don't rub people's noses in it. Disagreements about priorities are inevitable at work and at home because priorities reflect character. I might believe the most important thing I can do in a business deal is get the best possible terms for myself. That priority is driven by a lack of generosity. I might also think getting the deal done is what's most important and the terms don't matter; that's driven by too much generosity or rashness. If I'm a coward, I'll prioritize safety before anything. If I'm rash, I'll prioritize independence. Rather than take a priority difference head on, wait; people often forget. My father worked with a man who eventually became the secretary of defense. He kept ten stacks of papers across the front of his desk. This is back when having a lot of paper on your desk showed how busy you were. Whenever this man was given a task, he put the request in the pile on the far left side of his desk, and each day he moved the request into the next pile. When he looked through the pile on the far right, the last pile, if no one had asked him about the request since the first time it was made, he threw it out. That's one way to win an argument about priorities without having to argue.

Your Organization

Let's look at the chart from Chapter 5 again, but this time apply it to your organization. Circle the phrase or phrases in each row that best describe your organization. When you're done, each row should have either one or two phrases circled.

TABLE 10: YOUR ORGANIZATION

We're sometimes like this	We're always like this	We're sometimes like this
Your organization is fearful, lacks confidence and spirit, or is unable to make difficult decisions.	After considering risks, your organization takes actions and makes decisions that can have a negative impact on it for the benefit of something larger than itself.	Your organization takes stupid risks or overindulges in dangerous activities.
Your organization is over the top or out of control.	Your organization is not overoccupied with newness or distraction.	Your organization is unable to take pleasure from things.
Your organization is selfish and fearful with money.	Your organization shares money wisely, giving the right amount to the right people at the right time, without regard for getting credit or creating advantage for itself.	Your organization is thoughtless and overly casual with money.
Your organization is irritable, touchy, easily bothered, or can't take a joke.	Your organization is slow to anger, and when it gets angry, it's for the right reasons and directed at the right people in the right way.	Your organization won't defend itself.
Your organization is rude or thoughtless.	Your organization doesn't cause others pain by being rude or selfish, it doesn't flatter, and it doesn't debase itself to anyone.	Your organization flatters, manipulates, or fakes interest.
Your organization fakes humility or talks itself down.	Your organization clearly understands its qualities. It doesn't boast or talk itself down.	Your organization exaggerates its qualities; it bullshits about things it knows little about.
Your organization is dull or can't make a joke.	Your organization is charming and professional. Your organization isn't dull or silly.	Your organization is unprofessional.
Your organization has little drive or doesn't care about quality.	Your organization has a desire to earn honors for the right reasons. It wants to be recognized for excellence but not at the expense of character.	Your organization is a glory hound or a praise pig.

I have been happiest in my career when my character matched up well with my organization's character. I've been unhappy when my organization and I didn't have any virtues or vices in common. This step isn't just about embracing your virtues; it's about embracing all of your character, virtues and vices both. Your organization needs to do the same if it's going to improve. When an organization can't face its vices, it's just like a person who can't: stuck. I have to recognize my vices and manage them if I'm going to moderate them until they become virtues. I need my vices, and I'm lucky that they will never go away, because without them I would have no virtue.

Chapter in a Chart: Embrace Your Character—All of It

Ability with character ⬅ ▶	Ability alone
Wisdom	Intelligence
Einstein had to do a lot of math before he could create his famous equation. He needed courage to get through that.	Einstein couldn't dunk a basketball, but it didn't seem to bother him too much.
Ben Hogan spoke of not being born with a great golf swing but having to "dig it out of the dirt." In 1949 Hogan almost died in a car accident that broke his pelvis in two places. From 1950 to the end of his career he won six majors, including three in one year.	A player playing with Hogan is said to have hit a hole in one after Hogan teed off and landed on the green. While walking to the next hole, Hogan said to his playing partner who hit the hole in one, "That's the first time I ever birdied that hole."
I was asked to write a curriculum about how to write a consulting report. I didn't fret much about how it would be received; I just wrote the best curriculum I could.	I didn't think enough about the real needs of my audience.

Why it matters →	What to do about it
Intelligence—how fast you process and how much you can accurately infer—doesn't become wisdom until you apply character to it. We don't even need intelligence to be wise.	Don't let your intelligence or expertise get in the way of growing wise. Remind yourself daily that even the people you know well are a mystery, often to themselves. Accept people as they are, including yourself.
Talent brings responsibility. If you have the talent to find a cure for hunger but not the character to develop your talent, all humanity suffers.	Embrace what you're good at. Don't worry about what you're not good at. Honor your strengths by working to realize them. Humanity will thank you.
Excellence makes us selfish. Hogan needed to turn inward to win championships. Other golfers have eaten hot dogs and smoked cigars with the crowd between shots. Hogan couldn't do that. He never tried to be likable.	Don't be ashamed of your vices; be aware of them. Hogan might have scored just as well that day if he'd congratulated his playing partner. That he didn't does not make him evil.
I love what I wrote and still feel proud of it, but it became a running joke with the consultants who were supposed to benefit from it.	Do the work for yourself, but don't forget your audience. It's OK to be self-indulgent sometimes. Just edit it out before you go to print.

Practice Step 7

Hint: "You can only shape and improve your character if you embrace all of it—virtues and vices—because vices are just over- or underdeveloped virtues."

The scenario:

You work for a conservative, family-owned company. You report to someone who reports to one of the cofounders. You're not afraid of conflict and have a reputation as a courageous truth teller. Your organization is afraid of conflict, both with customers and internally.

One of your company's cofounders asks you to attend a meeting with your boss and your company's largest client. The cofounder says she wants you there because you have an expertise the client has expressed interest in. When the meeting starts, it becomes obvious that your boss and the client don't get along. This is bad because your boss is the client's primary contact within your organization. There's an awkward pause in the conversation where the client and your boss are frustrated with each other.

What should you do?

If you want to …

⊛ Try to break the tension with humor, go to page 161.

⊛ Stay silent, go to page 163.

TRY TO BREAK THE TENSION WITH HUMOR.

You say something about the awakened tension, but no one laughs. The cofounder groans in a way to say, "Bad joke," but doesn't acknowledge your comment further. The client looks out the window and says nothing. Your boss shoots you a look like, "We'll talk about this later."

Your company's cofounder turns the conversation toward progress made while acknowledging areas where the client is frustrated. After a few moments, she dismisses you and your boss and continues the meeting alone with the client. Your boss asks you to come back to her office, where she tells you not to use humor at work because it makes you look unprofessional.

Yikes. Can't anybody take a joke? Not when money is on the line. Humor can be a powerful tool in business, but it's not easy to pull off. (If no one shares your sense of humor where you work, you're probably working in the wrong place.) You may have the courage to acknowledge an awkward situation with a client, but your boss and your company's cofounder do not. You need to respect their reluctance and wait for a better time to become part of the conversation. Your company's cofounder invited you to the meeting because she thought you could help. Wait for the right moment before you speak.

STAY SILENT.

Your company's cofounder turns the conversation toward the progress your company is making with the client while acknowledging places where the client is frustrated. She then mentions the client's curiosity about your area of expertise and introduces you. The client says he thinks his organization may not be doing enough in your area, but he's not sure what the right things to do are, so he doesn't know.

What should you do next? Read "Step 8: Make a List of All the People around You Who Can Help You Succeed" to find out.

WHAT COMES NEXT

Growing your virtue and moderating your vice can't be done alone—at least I've never been able to do it. In the next chapter, you're going to make a list of everyone who can help you shape your character to get the most from your abilities. The list of people might be longer than you think.

Make a List of All the People around You Who Can Help You Succeed

Wonderful brilliance may be gained for our judgment by getting to know others. We are all huddled and concentrated in ourselves, and our vision is reduced to the end of our nose.
—MONTAIGNE

I love every person I meet, and most of them love me back.
—MARGARET THE PUG

Step 8 is an opportunity to think about who we want to learn from, and it's an obligation to talk to people who are a problem for us. The people who disagree with us are often the ones we learn the most from. Approaching them with sincerity takes humility. Even if they are not people of goodwill, it's best to be close to them so you can keep an

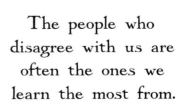

The people who disagree with us are often the ones we learn the most from.

eye on them. I had a colleague who completely got under my skin. He was higher up in the organization, so I had to deal with him. After listening more closely to what he was saying, which was always reasonable, and acknowledging and responding to his requests, even if my response was, "I can't do this now, but I can do it later," I began to learn from him. He became one of my closest friends and mentors.

Here's an example of what making a list of the people who can help you succeed looks like in practice. It's the story of the IT director who wanted to be invited to all your meetings.

The IT director needs to be on your list of people to talk to. There's a good chance he won't tell you why he wanted to come to all your meetings unless you ask him, and you need to ask him because your team needs his support to succeed. Don't put off a conversation now with the hope that the problem will fix itself. If it's a real problem, it won't fix itself, and if it's not a real problem, you'll feel relieved when you find that out. If the director avoids you, it may not be because of you; it may be because he doesn't like hard conversations any more than most people do. Don't let him escape without an answer.

You

You need to know what success means to you before you can start asking people to help get you there. Hopefully your conversions from "Step 6: Share Your Inventory with a Trusted Friend" helped you define success for yourself. The more clearly you can define what you want, the more helpful other people can be. Start your list of people to talk to by thinking about your immediate peers. For me, it's a list of all my clients and colleagues, past and present. Social capital—also known as "Who you know"—is as important as financial capital for success, and it's a renewable and inexhaustible resource. Your reputation is the key that unlocks the riches of social capital, so be the kind of person you would want to help. Your list of who can help you succeed might be quite long. In fact, it should be. Don't lack imagination when thinking about who can help you. Not everyone you know will be on your list. Some people are too difficult to work with, others have little to teach, but these should be the exceptions. As the saying goes, if you meet one jerk in a day, they're the jerk. If everyone you meet is a jerk, you're the jerk.

Your reputation is the key that unlocks the riches of social capital, so be the kind of person you would want to help.

Other People

People who can help you fall into two categories: people at work and people outside work.

People at work	People outside work
Subordinates	Friends
Superiors	Family
Peers	Colleagues
Clients	People you admire but don't know or don't know well

Why two different lists? Because we can't completely trust the people we work with. Money changes relationships. We need money to survive, so work relationships are partially about survival and always about power. Diplomats don't tell everything to their closest allies; we shouldn't tell everything to our work allies either. Work relationships should be founded on a positive vision for the future, not mutual suffering. We can complain to friends. Complaining at work is always a bad idea. Colleagues are categorized as outside of work even though you may know them through work because there's no money involved in those relationships, just potential money. It's easier to be intimate when no money is at stake.

Who do you admire and want to get to know better? Put them on your list. They are the most important people in your development. You can get to know them by reading their books or listening to their podcasts. They are easy to approach if you broadcast selflessness and genuine enthusiasm when you contact them, so put Peter Thiel and Bill Gates on your list if you want to. You just may not get a response. Keep your requests simple; sometimes the best thing someone can do is to introduce you to other people. A friend sent a note to a blogger who was often quoted in business journals. The blogger posted about my friend's work, and a string of articles in major publications about my friend's work was the long-term effect of one email.

Be patient when you approach new people. These conversations can be the beginning of lifelong relationships. Very few people want to get married after the first date.

Your Organization

People like the Interrupting Salesperson should be on your list of people who can help you succeed. If someone is a successful salesperson, they probably know something worth learning. You need to understand how they approach their work and how they think about your products. Most of the decision makers and influencers in your organization should also be on your list. Getting into meaningful conversations with each of them can be the work of a career. Have patience. You don't want to schedule a one-on-one with the CEO your first week on the job as a junior associate at a multinational.

Here's a chart to help prioritize who to talk to depending on the status of your product:

GOLD

TABLE 11: SOURCES OF INFORMATION BASED ON THE STATUS OF YOUR PRODUCT

	Status of Your Product		
	Growing: product works and you get referral business	**Stalled: sales are slow, product is awkward, and there's little customer enthusiasm**	**Newborn: product is unproven, few referrals, and you're selling an idea**
Best source and why	**Sales** Salespeople should be able to tell you why people buy. That's critical to know at this stage, and it may not be why you think.	**Customer Support** Customer support can be geniuses about a product's unrealized potential. You have to realize potential to pull out of the stall.	**Customers and Prospects** Prospects who say, "I don't need this," can be your best sources. Find out what they do need, make what they need your own, and sell that.
"Meh" source and why	**Customer Support** Even if a product is perfect, Customer Support will hear about problems. If Customer Support can tell you why people are buying, that's great. If not, take things with a grain of salt.	**Product Development** Product development issues might be why the product is stalled. The people who created a problem are rarely the right people to solve it.	**Founders** Founders are stubborn by nature. Stubbornness is not helpful when you're looking for a product/market fit, but perseverance is.
Bad source and why	**Product Development** Many product developers can only talk about the product; they have little understanding of how the product is used or why it's valuable to customers. If the product is working, product development ... want to make it ...er, and that instinct ...killed more products ...defects have.	**Sales** Sales will likely blame marketing if the product is stalled. It's more likely stalled because you don't understand your buyers and what they need. That's an "everybody" problem, not just marketing.	**Marketing** At this stage marketing is making things up. They might know what messages and offers prospects are engaging with, but those messages might be beyond your true capabilities.

The objective of these interviews is to find concrete, simple things you can do to make things better for your customers and your organization. If you do that, things will get better for you too.

Chapter in a Chart: Make a List of All the People around You Who Can Help You Succeed

People who can help you succeed	People who can't
People who have something you want.	Anyone you don't ask.
Friends who work like you want to.	Friends whose work habits you'd rather avoid.
People you admire who you don't know.	People who want to sell something to you.
People who know someone you want to know.	People who don't respect you.
Anyone who likes you or needs something from you.	People who know nothing about you.
Anyone who feels like they're working alone when they're working in a group.	People who think only their work matters.

Why it matters	What to do about it
Someone only needs to have one thing you want to be able to help you, and no answer to a request is worse than being refused. At least with a refusal, you know where you stand.	You have to ask for the sale. The worst anyone can say is nothing, because "No" is so much more helpful than silence. If you don't ask, all you hear is nothing.
We play up or down to the level of the people we play with.	Stick with the winners. You'll play your best game when you play with people who are better than you.
Don't be transactional with anyone, particularly people you want to make a good impression on, and don't let anyone treat you like a transaction either.	Find people who are nearing the end of their career. They are often in a generous mood.
People who love you may want to show you off.	Take advantage of the networks of your peers and treat every introduction respectfully.
There are more people in your corner than you know, and you can add more if you ask the right way.	Frequently update your list of people who can help you succeed. Your list should always be growing. Reading it can be encouraging in dark times.
Many of us never see how others use our work. Helping others see how their work is useful is a great kindness.	It's OK to end a conversation that has stopped being interesting or productive. Just be courteous so as not to poison future communications.

Practice Step 8

Hint: "More people love you than you know, including people you haven't met yet, and all of them can help you."

The scenario:

One of your company's cofounders asks you to attend a meeting with your company's largest client. Your boss will also be there. When the meeting starts, it becomes obvious that your boss and the client don't get along. This is bad because your boss is the client's primary contact within your organization. There's an awkward pause in the conversation where the client and your boss are frustrated with each other when your company's cofounder turns the conversation toward the progress your company is making with the client. She mentions the client's curiosity about your area of expertise and introduces you. The client says he thinks his organization may not be doing enough in your area, but he's not sure what the right things to do are, so he doesn't know.

How should you respond?

If you want to …

⊛ Ask why the client thinks he can do more, go to page 179.

⊛ Talk about best practices in your area, go to page 181.

ASK WHY THE CLIENT THINKS HE CAN DO MORE.

The client smiles. "That's a good question. It's mostly a feeling. I suppose it's because we're not seeing the results we want." You ask a few more questions and find out the client has not implemented even the basic foundations of your area of expertise and has no idea how to begin. It's disturbing because this is not a new client, and they should be further along than this.

What should you do?

If you want to say …

- "We can definitely help you. We have an evaluation process that would be a good place to start," go to page 183.

- "Let me circle back with (the names of your cofounder and your boss) and get back to you with suggestions," go to page 185.

TALK ABOUT BEST PRACTICES IN YOUR AREA.

You start to go through some of the basics of your area of expertise when your boss interrupts you. "We've been over these things before," he says. Your cofounder nods in agreement and says, "I think we'd be better off learning more about what (name of the client) wants."

Yikes. Not a good outcome. Can't you talk about what you know? Of course you can, but now is not a good time. Launching into a conversation about best practices is a bit like saying you're smarter than everyone in the room. That might be true, but it's embarrassing to your boss and your company's cofounder. You need to learn more and earn more trust before you show off what you know.

Your boss and your company's cofounder should be near the top of your list of people who can help you succeed. You need to prioritize your relationships with them. They brought you into the meeting to be a bright, shiny thing with a client who's frustrated. Don't try to solve everything in one conversation. Say just enough to be fascinating and nothing more. The best outcome for you is to add the client to your list of people who can help you succeed while building goodwill with your boss and the cofounder.

If you want to try again, go to "Practice Step 8" on page 177.

"WE CAN DEFINITELY HELP YOU. WE HAVE AN EVALUATION PROCESS THAT WOULD BE A GOOD PLACE TO START."

This is a good answer if you work in an aggressive company; you're trying to close a sale. You also might make the client happy with this response. He admitted he doesn't know what he's doing in your area, and that takes courage, so you might make a good pair with him, but you'll never get the chance if your boss and cofounder are uncomfortable with the idea.

You work in a conservative, family company. There's always an emotional context in a family company, and you may not be enough of an insider yet to understand it. It's better to go slow and bring your boss and your cofounder along.

If you want to try again, go to "Practice Step 8" on page 177.

"LET ME CIRCLE BACK WITH (THE NAMES OF YOUR COFOUNDER AND YOUR BOSS) AND GET BACK TO YOU WITH SUGGESTIONS."

The meeting ends well. The client seems to like you, and your boss and your cofounder look relieved. But all is not well. There's still friction between your largest client and your boss.

To find out what to do about it, read "Step 9: Speak with All the People on Your List to Learn What They Need to Succeed" to learn what they need to succeed.

WHAT COMES NEXT

In the next chapter you'll learn to play journalist so you can find out what people need to succeed. Knowing that will give you great power to drive your own success.

Speak with All the People on Your List to Learn What They Need to Succeed

Let (the student) be taught above all to surrender before truth
as soon as he perceives it, whether it be found in the hands
of his opponents or in himself through reconsideration.
—MONTAIGNE

Tom needs to be loved, and by loving him I get everything I want.
—MARGARET THE PUG

There are so many people who can help us. It's often a lack of confidence or imagination, or sometimes it's pride that prevents us from asking. Don't get emotional about needing other people's help. Step 9 is about fact finding. You'll interview people to understand their motivations, like a reporter collecting facts. The more facts you have, the better you'll be able to influence people to get what you need. Remember that love can be self-interest rightly understood. It's not a sin to help someone else because it feels good. It's also not a sin to help someone else because it gives you power.

You

Knowing what other people need brings you closer to the truth of your character.[6] Can you really help someone, or do you only want to help yourself through them? If you learn to enjoy learning about others, without thinking about how they can help you, you'll learn to enjoy life. You can practice by talking to the checkout person in the grocery or the mailman. My brother-in-law met his wife by complimenting her on her shoes while riding in an elevator. Genuine interest in others is not self-centered schmoozing; it's an act of love. If you show real interest in everyone, no matter whether they can help you or not, you'll build a great talent for relationships based on love. Many of those relationships can also help you in business. The helping-in-business part is a happy by-product and not the object of showing interest in others. To know how to advance your own agenda, you need to understand the agendas of others, and loving others is a good way to do that.

Other People

We all die someday, so there's no point in being afraid of anyone. We're equal, and no one's judgment matters but your own. People in

---

6   I find it hard to lie to myself for long. Near the end of my drinking, I pledged a fraternity in college after promising myself I wouldn't. It didn't end well; I had a fit during a pledge training activity and quit so dramatically that the chapter called an emergency meeting to discuss if pledge training needed to be reformed. I was the problem, not pledge training. I was trying to force my heart into a place it didn't fit. We can't fool ourselves without costs. "It is for slaves to lie and for free men to speak truth." — Montaigne, quoting Apollonius

positions of power rarely understand this. If you understand it, you'll always have an advantage over people in power, because they won't be able to divert you from what you know is right. When you understand someone's motivations, goals, and fears, it's easier to influence them. Speak with people to learn what they need so you can align it with what you need. It's their needs, but it's your agenda.

When you speak to people on your list, make the conversation about them and your role, not about you personally. The more facts you have about what people need, the better you'll be able to influence them. Be like a reporter. Interview to understand motivations, and never make the conversation about you. Here are some questions you might use:

- ⊛ What does success look like for you?

- ⊛ How are you measured?

- ⊛ Do you get a bonus? What do you have to do to earn your bonus?

- ⊛ What information is important to you in your work? Is there important information you struggle to get?

- ⊛ What are your expectations for the people in my role? How can we help you?

Create a chart that maps stakeholders to their needs. On the left side of the chart, list the people who can help you succeed. On the top line of the chart, create columns for each person's department, role, top need, secondary need, and everything else. The "everything else" column can have as many items as needed, but make people choose a top need and a second need. The sooner you begin teaching them that they can't get everything they want when they want it, the better.

If you work in the software business, your finished chart might look like this:

TABLE 12: EXAMPLE CHART OF WHAT PEOPLE NEED

	Department	Role	Top Need	Second Need	Everything Else
Patrick	Sales	Individual Contributor	Qualified leads	Differentiating features	• Product road map • Industry trends • Competitive intelligence
Megan	Marketing	Manager	Reliable release dates	Differentiating features	• Customer stories • Industry trends • Competitive intelligence
Sree	Technology	Manager	Commitment from leadership to fix things that are broken	Requirements	More resources
Cynthia	Customer Success	Leader	Defects to be fixed	Reliable release dates	Product road map

You may need to ask the same question in more than one way to get the complete answer. You can ask, "What's your top need?" and "What does success look like for you?" and then compare the answers.

Your actions after the interviews are critical to your credibility. There's no point for the interviewees to share their needs with you if you don't take action on their needs. You don't have to do everything you learn about, but you need to make visible progress if you want to grow your influence. Look for common threads across interviews and create a prioritized to-do list that will make you a hero if you complete the first two or three items, because so many people want those things to get done.

TABLE 12: WHAT PEOPLE NEED

Person	Department	Role	Top Need	Second Need	Everything Else

Your Organization

After you talk to people, analyze their needs to match them up with what people in your function should be doing for the organization. You need to understand your own role to do this, but you can still analyze your interviews even if you're not quite sure what you ought to be doing in your role. Make a second chart that aligns what people need with what you can do in your role. This goes back to the "What should I be doing in my role?" question, and it's an essential question no one can answer for you. You have to take your role and remake it in your own image to be a standout success. On the left side of the chart, write what you can do in your role. Across the top of the chart, write a column for the most popular top need that was identified in your interviews, another column for the second most popular need, and a third column for the third most popular top need. Then create a fourth column for the most popular second need and a fifth column for the second most popular second need.

> You have to take your role and remake it in your own image to be a standout success.

After you've written what people need across the top of the chart and what you can do in your role in the far-left column, decide how well what you do supports what people need. For instance, if people most need food, and you can cook food, what you do strongly supports what people need. If you can keep books as an accountant, what you can do may only indirectly support people who need to eat. The chart below is an example from the point of view of someone who works as a product manager. Your chart should reflect the needs you identified in your interviews and your own skills.

EXAMPLE OF MAPPING WHAT YOU DO TO WHAT PEOPLE NEED

	Most popular top need	Second most popular top need	Third most popular top need	Most popular second need	Second most popular second need
	Reliable release dates	Defects fixed	Commitment to fix what's broken	Differentiating features	Address customer requests
Prioritization	Low support	Strong support	Strong support	Strong support	Strong support
Requirements gathering	Strong support	Low support	Strong support	Indirect support	Strong support
Competitive intelligence	No support	No support	No support	Strong support	No support
Product positioning	No support	No support	Indirect support	Indirect support	Low support
Customer interviews	No support	Low support	Indirect support	Low support	Strong support

Things people in my role do

The purpose of this analysis is to determine how well your role aligns with what people need. If there's weak alignment, you need to redefine your role. If there's strong alignment, you know what you need to do to succeed. Use the information from your interviews to make connections and form alliances with people who need the same things, particularly people who need the same things you need. Most organizations—even small organizations—require at least some consensus before they will take action. Consensus isn't democracy; all votes and voices are not equal. Decision makers will bend to pressure if the group pushing for the change is committed enough. With the intelligence you collected through your interviews, you'll be better equipped than anyone—even the CEO—to create consensus, because you'll see alignments and misalignments others aren't aware of.

Unless you have greater formal authority than the person you disagree with, most arguments in business are won through coalition building. Even if you win because you're the stronger opponent, your track record for decisions had better be good if you want good people to follow you. Continuously ignoring the arguments of weaker opponents and being wrong about your decisions is doubly damaging, far more than simply being wrong. It's better to be open-minded and wrong than stubborn and wrong.

Chapter in a Chart: Speak with All the People on Your List to Learn What They Need to Succeed

When you ask people what they need ...	When you tell people what you need ...
... you lay the foundation for a relationship based on trust.	... you make them defensive.
... you gain information that can make you powerful.	... you limit your options.
... you take a step toward loving people at work.	... you make the relationship about you.
... you can align other people's agendas with your own.	... you can create resistance for no reason.
... you learn.	... you presume to know.

Why it matters ◀━━━▶	What to do about it
It's hard to live a happy life if people don't trust you. Doing something that needs to be done without being asked is both leadership and service, and it builds trust.	Follow up on the things people tell you they need. Give status updates, even if the update is "I haven't gotten to it yet." Anticipate needs where you can.
Most of us don't know our own hearts. We have to learn what makes us happy through other people.	Look outside yourself for happiness. Help others without regard for how it will help you.
We don't have to enjoy what we do to love the people we do it with. Very few people love combat, but many love the people they experienced combat with.	Ask how you can help in a way that doesn't sound like, "How can I help you help me?"
Sales, marketing, technology, support, and product probably don't report to you, but you need work from all of them to be successful.	Always be working on a hard problem, but throw some easy wins on your to-do list to show visible progress. Sometimes an easy win will make a hard problem go away.
The more facts you have, the better you'll be able to influence people to get what you need.	Talk to everyone to grow the list of people who can help you succeed.

Practice Step 9

Hint: "You get more from listening to someone than by talking to them."

The scenario:

One of the cofounders of the family business where you work invited you to a meeting with your boss and your company's largest client. Your boss and the client don't get along. In fact, they annoy each other. You have an expertise the client is interested in. You told the client you would discuss how you could help with your boss and the cofounder.

What should you do next?

If you want to …

⊛ Ask the cofounder if you can replace your boss as the manager of the client, go to page 203.

⊛ Wait for your boss or the cofounder to make the next move, go to page 205.

ASK THE COFOUNDER IF YOU CAN REPLACE YOUR BOSS AS THE MANAGER OF THE CLIENT.

You're able to get some time alone with just you and the cofounder. "Thanks for the invite to the meeting," you begin. "I'm happy to take over the account."

"Why would you take over the account?" asks the cofounder.

"I can see (the name of your boss) and (the client's name) don't get along," you respond.

"Why do you say that?" asks the cofounder. You're a little shocked. It seemed obvious to you, but the cofounder doesn't see things that way. "Nobody's asking you to take over anything. Just stay in your lane and do your job."

Ouch. How did that happen? Offering to take over the account may be the right move in a different organization, but not the organization that's in this scenario. This is a conservative, family business that's conflict averse. You need to listen to people more and find out what they need to succeed before you can offer solutions. You have the right solution in mind, but that's not enough to fix the problem. You need to make other people think it's their idea to have you manage the account. They might already be thinking that, but they need you to help them make the move.

If you want to try again, go to "Practice Step 9" on page 201.

WAIT FOR YOUR BOSS OR THE COFOUNDER TO MAKE THE NEXT MOVE.

It's against your nature, but you decide the best thing to do right now is wait for your boss or the cofounder to talk with you about the meeting with the client. You don't have to wait long, as your boss sends you a note to ask how everyone should follow up with the client.

How should you respond? To find out, read "Step 10: Take a Daily Inventory."

WHAT COMES NEXT

Now that you've spoken with people to find out what they need, it's time to get to work helping them. To do that to the best of your ability, you need to take a daily inventory of your actions. We'll talk about how to do that next.

Take a Daily Inventory

Things at birth are imperfect; they gain in
size and strength as they grow.
—MONTAIGNE

I never make the same mistake twice. They're all a little different.
—MARGARET THE PUG

To get better at something, we have to practice and get feedback. This includes shaping our character. A daily inventory is like self-coaching for character development. If you take a daily inventory, you'll be better prepared to deal with challenges like this:

You've been assigned to lead a project that's critical for your organization. The chief revenue officer (CRO) is the executive sponsor. You've scheduled the project kickoff meeting with the team and the CRO. The CRO's schedule is a nightmare, and the lead developer's isn't much better, so just getting the meeting on the calendar feels like a victory. You have a general idea about the project, but you and the CRO have not been able to get together to go over things in detail yet.

You log into the meeting a few minutes early so you can greet the team as they come in. Just then you get a text from the CRO: "Can't make the meeting. Go on without me."

What should you do?

Are you capable of running this meeting by yourself, or do you need to reschedule? That depends on how you react when something unexpected and frustrating happens and what you broadcast to the people around you when it happens. If you take a daily inventory and review it regularly to identify patterns, you can react to this challenge based on real data and not just on impulse.

You

There are lots of ways to take a daily inventory. I use a combination of things I learned in recovery and things I read. My template looks like this:

TABLE 13: DAILY INVENTORY TEMPLATE

What do I want to get done today?

What did I do?

What do I feel good about?

What do I regret?

I write in the "What do I want to get done today?" column when I wake up. I fill out the other columns at night when I go to bed. I use an online database for my daily inventory to make analysis easier, but paper is great too. If you make up your own template, keep it simple, or you won't do it. Consistency is more important than completeness with an inventory.

I start my inventory with what I want to get done, but that's not essential. Inventories are not to-do lists. To-do lists make us feel good, but they're meaningless; real progress doesn't come from crossing things off a list. "OK, I've achieved maximum wittiness, so I can cross that one off the list!" Real progress comes from discipline. If a to-do

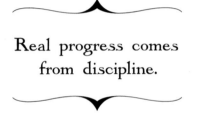

Real progress comes from discipline.

list helps you develop discipline, use one, but don't confuse crossing things off a list with discipline. Discipline isn't busyness; it's action informed by reflection. When I review my list at night, I'm mostly concerned with what I thought I would do when I started the day but didn't get done. Are there things I'm avoiding? Are there things I put on my list because I think I'm supposed to do them? I keep my to-do list short and general. Detailed to-do lists are helpful for lots of things, but not for character building. Some days I actually do everything on the list. Those are good days, even if I only put three things on the list.

Here's what a daily inventory looks like for me after I've finished it at the end of the day:

TABLE 14: SAMPLE DAILY INVENTORY

What do I want to get done today?

- *Write for book*
- *Market for business*
- *Exercise*
- *Work for clients*

What did I do?

- *Write for book*
- *Market for business*
- *Work for clients*

What do I feel good about?

- *New connections that could lead to good opportunities.*
- *Good progress on Chapter 10*

What do I regret?

- *No exercise*
- *Forgot to walk the dog*

Examining regrets is great for building new disciplines and reinforcing old ones. The voice that tells me I have a regret is a very helpful voice. I listen to it so I can limit my regrets. If I never regretted anything, I'd either be a narcissist or a psychotic. We should all have some regrets, even little ones, like "Oh, I wish I ordered what you ordered." I don't want to live in regret, but I hope I never stop having a few regrets, because they teach me something important. Most of my regrets are about things I didn't do, like exercise. Regretting that I don't exercise may mean that I'm a bad planner, or it may mean I don't really want to exercise and only regret that I didn't exercise because I think I'm supposed to exercise.

If something keeps showing up on your list as a regret, and you do nothing about it, it's either a big issue or not a real regret; it's just something you think you're supposed to do but don't want to do. Stop beating yourself up and let it go; if it's important, you'll come back to it.

Other People

After I think about myself, I think about how I acted toward other people. Did I hurt anyone that day? This includes everyone I meet or talk to; as they say, "You can learn a lot about a person by the way they treat waiters." My youngest son taught me the importance of extending courtesy to everyone when I bit the head off a phone solicitor who called me about DirecTV. I answered the phone in the car while circling the airport. When I hung up, my son said, "Dad! You were so rude to that guy. That's his job. Imagine how hard that job must be." He was right, and I was ashamed, so now I try to live up to what he said. We can extend love or no love with any action. No-love actions don't mean, "I hate you. Get away from me." They mean, "I don't care about you," and they're pathetic. Don't be pathetic; make the effort to care. If you keep an inventory of the small hurts you cause, you won't cause many big hurts.

I added some columns to my inventory to track how I acted with other people:

TABLE 15: EXPANDED DAILY INVENTORY TEMPLATE

What do I want to get done today?

What did I do?

What do I feel good about?

What do I regret?

> **Was I kind and loving toward all?**

> **Do I owe an apology?**

I'm a big fan of kindness. Kindness comes in many forms, but it never comes as weakness. Montaigne had disdain for "the common herd," but he was never rude. I love this passage from his essay "Of Friendship":

> I scarcely inquire of a lackey whether he is chaste; I try to find out whether he is diligent. And I am not so much afraid of a gambling mule driver as of a weak one, or of a profane cook as of an ignorant one. I do not make it my business to tell the world what it should do—enough others do that— but what I do in it.

Allowing others to be who they are as long as who they are does you no harm seems a great sort of kindness. I can be kind and loving just by being tolerant and polite.

The last column, "Do I owe an apology?" is the hardest one for me. If I think I owe an apology to everyone, I'm an egotist: the world is all about me. If I never owe an apology to anyone, I'm not trying hard enough. Some days I write, "Not yet," in this column because I'm still thinking things over. An apology that comes close after an offense is better than one that comes long after, but a late apology is better than none if one is required.

Your Organization

How can you fire someone in a kind and loving way? It's not easy, but it can be done. I was at a company that had a layoff after poor financial performance. The CEO didn't say it was a layoff; he said it was a "purification." That was cowardly and unkind, although he was normally a kind person. There are legal considerations for how honest we can be when someone has to be fired, but those should be faced and dealt with. Not firing someone who's making other people miserable is also unkind. If you're a manager, you should know who is making it and who isn't. If you don't try to help the people who aren't making it, you aren't being kind. Sometimes the last kind thing you can do for someone who isn't making it is to let them go.

Apologies at work can be a helpful start, but they are not required to take responsibility, and taking responsibility is much more important than being sorry. I have an old boss who summarized what a daily inventory about work is all about: "Did we do what we said we were going to do?" I like that he said "we" to include the whole organization. Customers don't differentiate between roles like, "You get a pass for ignoring me because you're in operations. If you were in sales, it would be a different thing." No. Everyone represents the company.

My daily inventory about work is simple: Did I do what I said I was going to do, and did I put in an honest day's work? The second part, "an honest day's work," varies. Sometimes I need to get away from work so I can think about work. I don't think well when I'm busy; lots of people are like that. I owe my employer my care but not my loyalty, and they don't owe me any loyalty either. After I'm paid, we're all even.

There are many simple inventories that are hugely helpful with work. Montaigne wrote about how his father had his steward add notable occurrences like who came for a visit, what special events happened, and other simple observations to his journal of accounts. We often don't know what's important when it happens. That's why it's good to keep track of simple, small things, and look for patterns. Accounting doesn't have to be about money; it can be about what happened in your life as well.

Chapter in a Chart: Take a Daily Inventory

An inventory is ...	An inventory isn't ...
Practice for dealing with conflict and hardship	Separate from your real life
A simple, honest appraisal of what you did that day	Beating yourself up or letting yourself off
A discipline to moderate your vices and nurture your virtues	A penance
A way to define love and kindness for yourself	Judging yourself by the standards of another
A way to keep track of your commitments	A contest to see how many things you can cross off your list

Why it matters	What to do about it
Instinct only takes us so far. We get better at things we practice and reflect on.	Make your inventory simple and do it as often as you can. Every day is best.
Telling yourself you're bad or great doesn't make you bad or great, but it can make you dull.	Be honest and kind with yourself and work to get better.
Virtue is the key to enduring happiness, happiness that lasts through trials and leaves a legacy behind after we die.	Look for patterns when you analyze your inventories. Share what you find with someone you love.
You need to decide what you want from your life.	Make a deliberate choice. Don't stumble into a life you don't want, and if you do, change it.
How many commitments we make isn't important. What kinds of commitments we make and how well we keep them is important.	Don't make many commitments, and keep the ones you do make.

Practice Step 10

Hint: "Being busy and making progress are very different. 'I am happier today than I was before' is progress. Busyness is distraction."

The scenario:

Your boss sent you a note to ask how you should handle a major client who is unhappy with progress. Your boss and the client don't get along. You've considered asking the cofounder of your conservative, family business to replace your boss with you as the client account manager, but you know that kind of aggressive play won't go over well in your conflict-averse organization. You have expertise in an area where the client is far behind. You also know the client has no idea how to improve in your area.

What should you do?

If you want to ...

⊛ Ask your boss if he wants you to write a proposal for services in your area of expertise for the client, go to page 225.

⊛ Suggest a follow-up call with the client, go to page 227.

ASK YOUR BOSS IF HE WANTS YOU TO WRITE A PROPOSAL FOR SERVICES IN YOUR AREA OF EXPERTISE FOR THE CLIENT.

Your boss tells you to go ahead and write the proposal and send it to the client. It's a lot of work and derails your day, but you get the proposal written and send it as an email, copying your boss and the cofounder. A few days go by, and you hear nothing. You send a note to the client, asking for feedback. Nothing. You go to your boss.

"Did you hear anything about the proposal I sent?" you ask.

"I didn't hear anything, but I asked about it when I spoke to the client just now," your boss says. "They're not interested."

"Any feedback about why?" you ask.

"They don't need it," your boss says. You know that's not true. So why was the proposal turned down?

It's hard to sell something new to a customer who is unhappy with what they already purchased. Your boss probably knows this and may have said it's OK for you to send a proposal, knowing the client would reject it. The rejected proposal gets you out of the conversation, and if your organization loses the client, it looks less like it's his fault.

Needing help and knowing you need help are very different. You haven't talked with your client or your boss enough to educate them about why they need your expertise. You need to learn more about what success looks like to your boss and your client before people will take your proposal seriously.

SUGGEST A FOLLOW-UP
CALL WITH THE CLIENT.

"Why would I want to talk to that guy?" asks your boss.

"It's pretty obvious you guys don't get along," you say. "You can't avoid him. He's our biggest client. Sometimes you just have to keep talking, and an answer will present itself."

"OK," your boss says. "And you want to be in the meeting?"

"Yes," you answer. "We said we'd follow up, so I need to be there," being sure to say "we" so you include everyone who was in the first meeting—you, your boss, and your cofounder—and "I" so your boss knows you're serious about being there.

"What do you want to talk about?" your boss asks.

Read "Step 11: Improve Your Insight through Contact with Customers, Colleagues, and People You Admire" to find out how you should answer.

WHAT COMES NEXT

In this chapter, you learned about taking inspiration from yourself by tracking progress with a daily inventory. In the next chapter, you'll learn about getting inspiration from others.

Improve Your Insight through Contact with Customers, Colleagues, and People You Admire

Truth and reason are common to everyone, and no more belong to the one who first spoke them than to the one who says them later.
—MONTAIGNE

All dogs are idiots. I alone am Margaret.
—MARGARET THE PUG

Wisdom and insight are wonderful things, but they don't come automatically; you have to work for them. Lightning comes from somewhere; spontaneous insights have typically been brewing in our minds for ages. Wisdom and insight don't have to be original to be valuable. In fact, it's better to have good taste than to be original. Have you ever been for a walk and found somewhere that seemed so pure and desolate that you thought you must be the only person to have been there? Then you find a candy wrapper or a cigarette butt, and the feeling is spoiled. The place hasn't changed, only your idea about it. We spoil insights the same way we spoil special places; we're jealous that the place is not ours alone. What does it matter? It's yours now. Use it.

You can use everything that happens to you to make you wiser, even things you hate, because everything that happens to you is part of a pattern. A counterexample is as instructive as a positive one, and studying it can help you find the next part of the pattern. You don't have to love something to be inspired by it. If you did, you could never learn from mistakes, since most of us hate mistakes. Let's look at how irritating things can lead to important insights.

> You don't have to love something to be inspired by it. If you did, you could never learn from mistakes, since most of us hate mistakes.

You come out of a meeting with your technology team and the director of IT. The director was in the meeting because he asked to be invited to all your meetings, and you complied. The director didn't say anything in the meeting and was on the phone most of the time. It's irritating, but you need to find out why the director wanted to be there, so you ask, "Do you have a few minutes to talk?"

The director nods. "I hear you have a problem with my team," he says.

"The team is fine. I have a problem with our performance," you say, because you know enough not to take what the director is doing personally.

The director smiles. "What do you think the problem is?"

"It feels like something is going on that I'm not aware of," you say. It's a good response because you're not presuming to know why the director wanted to come to the meeting, and you're not demanding to know why. Instead you've created an opening the director can use to tell you more.

The director sighs. "There is something, but I can't really talk about it," he says. "The team is floundering with technical issues that shouldn't take so much time. After code review, they're having to rewrite a lot of code to bring it up to spec. That shouldn't be happening, but we're working on it. I just need everyone to be patient."

You learned a lot in the exchange. You learned there's a sensitive issue with someone on the team that the director can't talk about, which means it's probably a human resources (HR) issue. You also learned the director doesn't know how to deal with the issue; if he did, he wouldn't need to come to the meeting. With those two pieces of information, you have the power to get your team what it needs if you can align your request with the HR issue the director is trying to solve. You've also learned from the director how not to act when you have an HR issue with someone. The director of IT is acting as if he has a special secret he can't share, but he told you what the secret is: the team is floundering with technical issues that shouldn't be issues. If you have something you have to keep in confidence, don't tell people that you have something you must keep in confidence. Either invite people into your trust or stay quiet about it.

You

There are answers inside you that you can't force out. You have to let them percolate. Walking, sitting, meditating, writing, and sleeping are all vital activities for finding answers inside yourself. You need patience. Most people want answers right away when they have problems, and the rush to answers can lead to terrible decisions. Why do people get divorced in the middle of their lives? Was the first half of their life a mistake? Perhaps. People change and fall out of love, but it's possible they're looking outside of themselves for a solution to a problem that's inside themselves. Getting old is hard, but it's also wonderful. I let go of things I don't need. Age whittles me down to my essentials. As my hair falls out and my body ages, I become happier, more confident, and less anxious, because I'm more accepting of myself. The acceptance comes through quiet reflection. You are a critical source of insight for your life, but you won't find the insight if you're always rushing about.

> You are a critical source of insight for your life, but you won't find the insight if you're always rushing about.

Meditation and quiet reflection are simple but not easy. As far as I know, there's no wrong way to meditate, but there are many ways to get little out of it. Meditation has more in common with playing a sport than it does with sleeping. Listen to the sounds around you. Bring your attention to your breathing. Quiet your mind, but don't smother it. All these things are easier said than done. Your challenges will change; some days you'll get sleepy during meditation or right after. Other days you won't find any quiet in your mind. But even the distractions have something to teach you, so don't fight against them too much. Many hours of unsatisfying practice might be rewarded with a single insight that makes all the effort worth it, but it's more likely that you'll make slow progress over a very long time. Meditation and reflection are still work even if you're sitting still, so sometimes they'll feel like drudgery. Stay consistent.

Other People

You have every thinker, artist, philosopher, writer, mogul, musician, businessperson, and rogue available to you to learn from. The entire history of civilization and almost all of science are only a keyboard and internet connection away. I'm ashamed of how I waste my time on the internet. How I recharge is very inefficient, and the quality of my company is embarrassing. What do I care about Kate and William when I could be spending time with George Burns and Gracie Allen, or Mike Nichols and Elaine May? Kate looks great in a hat, but other people have more to say. Choose your company wisely. You can still refresh yourself and be better for the time spent.

Here's a very partial list of people and things who've inspired me.

TOM'S ABRIDGED LIST OF SOURCES FOR INSIGHT

Who	What they did	What I learned from it
My father	Married my mother. Disciplined me gently. Supported me generously. Cofounded a business and provided a good living for hundreds of families over forty years.	How to be a good man, and if you're a person like him or like me, it's so much more fun to do your own thing than to work for someone else.
My wife	Married me. Loves me. Raised our children with me. Made a home for me.	By living for others we find ourselves. You can do great work in a short time if you take care with little things. The best people are both very serious and very funny. Life can be better than you can imagine.

Who	What they did	What I learned from it
Douglas Southall Freeman	Wrote an epic biography of George Washington. The abridged version is good too.	Energy is so important for building wealth. You can get angry and think petty thoughts and still be transformative if you keep your anger and pettiness to yourself. Stay out of personality clashes. Stay focused on the big stuff. Get other people to fight for your cause.
Stanley Kubrick	Cowrote and directed *2001: A Space Odyssey* and *Dr. Strangelove or: How I Learned to Stop Worrying and Love the Bomb.*	Humor and darkness are kissing cousins. It's better to maintain control of your vision than to be the richest.
Peter Thiel	Cofounded PayPal and cowrote my favorite business book, *Zero to One.*	If you want to make a lot of money, build a monopoly. You won't get much advantage if you think like everyone else, but being a contrarian is no guarantee of being right.
Bobby Frist	Cofounder and CEO of HealthStream	Treat everyone with respect. Have only a few intimates. Stay positive, and acknowledge that hard work is always required to do valuable things. Have clear principles and work them into your everyday language. Make your business about something more than money. Enjoy the struggle.
A large public company who was my customer	Pushed me to be better. Asked for the truth and listened without judging. Was always reasonable.	Hard customers make us better. If you tell the truth and take responsibility, you'll build credibility.
The game of golf	Humiliated me. Fascinated me. Relaxed me. Enraged me.	You will have more mediocre days than good days, but the good days are worth the effort. You can't think your way into right acting. As soon as you become too conscious of what you're doing, you'll ruin it.

Make a list of your sources for inspiration; it's easier to find more inspiration when you know what you're looking for. Going through your sources of inspiration is like going through your closet:

- "I like this sweater. Perhaps a shirt to go with it."

- "I like this thinker. Perhaps one of her influences would be good to try next."

Just about anything can be helpful to your practice, whether you're practicing business or something else. Train your eye to find the lessons.

Your Organization

If you can speak knowledgeably about customers, you'll build authority. The only way to speak knowledgeably about customers is to talk with customers. Often the people who use your product are not the people who buy it. You need to talk with users, their managers, and the people who pay for your product, or at least with the people in your organization who talk with those people, though that is a distant second best. In a business-to-business environment, direct connections to customers give people power, and people are often reluctant to share that power with others. You have to prove you'll do no harm before someone will share a customer contact with you. You also have to align whatever you want to talk about with something the person who owns the relationship cares about.

A formal customer advisory board is another way to get insight, but they're a lot of maintenance and sometimes not worth the trouble. Their value is often more symbolic than practical. User groups are also a good way to get feedback, but only if you let the user groups be managed by users and not by you. You won't get real feedback if your user groups are run by you, because people are reluctant to criticize the host. You can use software to collect data about your customers, but you still need to talk to buyers to understand their problems. Sometimes it's easier to ask than to interpret the data.

Expert networks are helpful though biased because you're paying for the privilege of talking to someone, and money changes everything. If you use one, think a lot about what you want to know before you start, and have some hypotheses about the market you want to test. Don't waste your time asking things like, "How much would you pay for this?" and "What don't you like about your current provider?" Those kinds of questions won't get you good data because the answers change all the time. Ask about enduring issues like culture and values, then do the thinking to connect their values with what you offer. Don't make your customers do your thinking for you. Finally, you can pay for consulting reports, but those are just table stakes; your competitors have them too. Your organization needs unique insights to gain an advantage.

It amazes me how hard it can be to win an argument when you start with, "We should do what's right for customers." Many organizations think little about customers; they think about their performance instead. Your performance will improve if you focus on your customers. Think of what you can do for them, and you'll be happier and more successful. It can be hard to do what's best for customers because customers can't tell you what's best for them because they don't know. Customers know problems; they don't know solutions. Solving customer problems in ways that show love is always the right choice if you want to live a happy life. Remember that love is a fair exchange of value; the more love we give, the more our reward, though the reward might be something other than money[7] and fame.

---

7   Money by itself is worthless. You need meaning to enjoy the freedom and choices money provides, and meaning comes from things other than money.

If we speak with customers openly, they'll tell us important things. Customers unlock solutions we can't dream up in committee. Listen to customers. Be an advocate for customers. Have curiosity about customers. Always seek to know them better because the better you know your customers, the more you can help them, and the more you help them, the more you'll profit.

Chapter in a Chart:
Improve Your Insight

You get insight when you ... ⟶	You stay ignorant when you ...
Sit in on sales calls and say nothing.	Talk about your products.
Read a lot, especially things unrelated to business.	Read the same things everyone else reads.
Cultivate friendships with people in other organizations at your career level or just a bit above you.	Talk only to people you work with.
Make friends with people nearing the end of their careers.	Talk only to your peers.
See things like a beginner.	Become too proud of your expertise.
Listen to people who disagree with you.	Listen to people you already agree with.

Why it matters ◀—▶	What to do about it
Your business can't survive without customers, but your customers can survive without you.	When you talk to customers, keep the conversation about them. Don't talk about your company or your products unless you're asked.
Every great idea in history is available to you if you make the effort.	Reduce the time you spend reading clickbait garbage and increase the time you spend reading things that make you think. Listen to books too.
Your next job offer likely will come from someone you don't know yet. I found one of my best bosses by saying hello to him in a swimming pool at a resort. We'd gone to school together but had never spoken there.	Seek out people and things you're truly interested in. Asking someone how they learned how to do something is flattering to them and educational for you.
You may be able to get access to people of a quality you could never reach otherwise. I met one of my mentors as he was leaving his consulting business, and I was starting mine. It was exciting for both of us.	Ask people you already know to introduce you to people they know. You don't need an agenda when you meet someone new; you can say you admire your mutual friend and want to meet more of their friends.
It's hard for experts to generate new ways to solve old problems because what they know gets in the way.	Be curious and humble. I worked with a world-famous cognitive psychology researcher who talked more about what he was learning than about what he knew.
Getting real, helpful feedback from people who like you can be a challenge. It could be that they see things as you see them. Or they may respond in a certain way because they don't want to hurt you.	A great way to turn a critic into a supporter is to invite them into your work. It's less appealing to crap on something you're sitting next to than to do it from a distance.

Practice Step 11

Hint: "Anyone can be your teacher. Even fools are right sometimes."

The scenario:

Your boss is responsible for your organization's largest client, and he's having trouble with the relationship; he and the client annoy each other. You know the client would benefit from your expertise, but you're not sure how to get the opportunity to help. After meeting the client in a meeting one of your company's cofounders invited you to, you suggested you and your boss have a follow-up conversation with the client. Your boss seems a bit skeptical about the idea.

"What do you want to talk about?" your boss asks.

How should you respond?

If you want to say ...

- ⊛ "I want to see if he would give us feedback about our products," then go to page 245.

- ⊛ "I want to hear more about what he's frustrated about," then go to page 247.

"I WANT TO SEE IF HE WOULD GIVE US FEEDBACK ABOUT OUR PRODUCTS."

"That seems pretty selfish," says your boss. "I don't think he'd want to do that. But I'll ask him the next time we talk." You go back to your office.

A few weeks go by, and you don't hear anything. Later, you get a note from the cofounder inviting you, your boss, and a few other people to a meeting to talk about why your largest customer, the one who was having trouble with your boss, is leaving. The CEO opens the meeting by saying, "I hold everyone here responsible for this loss, and it's unacceptable. I'll be making changes. I suggest you all take a good, hard look in the mirror and ask yourself where you screwed up. Send your thoughts to me by end of day."

Yikes. How did that happen? Your company's cofounder brought you into the meeting with the troubled client because of your expertise, but you never got the chance to show your expertise. Your boss is right that asking for feedback on your products sounds selfish when the customer is frustrated. A better conversation is to dig into the cause of the frustration and maybe let the customer vent. A great way to show expertise is to ask smart questions and show you're really listening and not just waiting to talk again. The client probably left because the cofounder and your boss are too conflict averse. People who are conflict averse can be very frustrating to more confrontational people. You have everything that's needed to save the account—you have the courage to speak plainly with the client, and you have expertise the client needs. That's all wasted if you can't get your boss to let you talk to the client.

If you want to try again, go to "Practice Step 11" on page 243.

"I WANT TO HEAR MORE ABOUT WHAT HE'S FRUSTRATED ABOUT."

"OK," says your boss. "I'll set up the meeting. Send me questions in advance you want to ask so I can steer the conversation. I'll send the invite after I get your questions."

Later that day you put your list of questions together. You focus on the client and what they're trying to achieve. You're careful not to ask anything that sounds like you're trying to qualify the client as a lead for a sale. Instead you ask questions a journalist might ask if they were learning about the business, things like, "How is your team measured?"; "What's a big worry for you right now?"; and "If you had a magic wand and could change one thing about your business, what would it be?"

During the phone call, you hit it off with the client. You and the client have a similar sense of humor, and you both like to say things that make other people a little uncomfortable. You don't get to ask many of your questions because the client takes the meeting as an opportunity to vent. By the end of the meeting, you're laughing, the client is laughing, and your boss is smiling.

After everyone hangs up, your boss speaks.

"I have a great idea," your boss says. "I think you should run this account. We can sync up so I stay in the loop. You can handle the day-to-day."

Great job! It was obvious you needed to run the account from the beginning, but you had to be patient and keep people talking to get there. You can learn from anyone, even if it's what not to do, and you got more from your boss and the client by listening than by talking.

Everyone likes a good listener. Be someone everyone likes.

WHAT COMES NEXT

Now that you're inspired, I hope you want to do something with your inspiration. You'll probably need other people to get it done. The next chapter is about getting things done by inspiring others to work with you.

Carry the Messages of Customer Love and Commitment to Improvement to Everyone You Meet

The gain from our study is to have become better and wiser by it.
—MONTAIGNE

I say nothing, and yet I'm loved.
—MARGARET THE PUG

If you want to lead, you need to be inspiring. You also have a duty to be inspiring even when you feel defeated yourself. The messages of customer love and commitment to make something great are messages worth carrying, no matter how tired you are, even if you have to carry them uphill against a headwind.

Let's look at an example where you need to carry the messages of customer love and commitment to improvement to get to a good outcome.

You were hard at work on an important announcement when you were interrupted by one of your company's best salespeople. The salesperson said they needed you to add an enhancement that hasn't been created yet to the next release of your product so he can land a deal. You learned the salesperson was having a call with the prospect in five minutes, so you asked if you could listen in. Now you're in the meeting with the salesperson and the prospect. The salesperson introduces you but indicates that he doesn't want you to talk. The call is about terms and conditions for the contract. The prospect seems eager to proceed. The enhancement the salesperson says he needs to close the deal never comes up.

What should you do?

You could do a lot of things after this meeting; you could think the whole meeting was a waste of time, and maybe even tell the salesperson he wasted your time. That helps no one—not even you—since it was your idea to come to the meeting. You could insist the enhancement isn't needed to close the deal since the subject never came up. You might be right, but you'll sound insulting; it's like telling the salesperson you know how to do their job better than they do. You and the salesperson have the same objective: find the simplest path to win the deal. That path does not include any new enhancements. Customer love and commitment to improvement means you have to find out why the customer needs the enhancement. Ask the salesperson why the enhancement never came up. In a conversation about terms and conditions, it should have if it's a real commitment.

You

If you want to be an example of love and commitment, you will need to control some of your natural reactions. It's natural to be irritated if you sit in on a dull meeting. Your irritation is self-centered. The less you think about yourself, the less other people will irritate you. Make your work about someone other than you. If you're a writer, think about your readers. If you're a software developer, think about the people who use your software. If you're a salesperson, think about your prospects. If a writer focuses on the words, he'll leave in a lot of words he likes that don't make the work better. If a software developer focuses on the software, the software will not be useful. If a salesperson focuses on closing the deal, the customer will not stay satisfied. If you think only of your work, you will lose track of why you do the work. You work to become better and wiser by it. Becoming better and wiser is entirely within your control. It does not depend on what results your work achieves. You are not just the manager of your

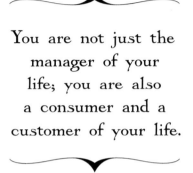

You are not just the manager of your life; you are also a consumer and a customer of your life.

life; you are also a consumer and a customer of your life. Carry the message of customer love and commitment to improvement to yourself. You will hear those messages loudest when you listen to others. You might listen to someone and hear, "I don't want to be like him." That's great; a counterexample is as helpful as a good one. You might listen to someone and hear, "That's the life I want." Even better, but be careful. You can't have someone else's life. You have to make your own. Their life might be a good model, but if you copy it, you'll lose yourself again. Cultivate good taste and follow your own tastes. They will inspire you.

Other People

Helping someone and giving them what they ask for are often different. Buyers put obstacles about why they can't buy in front of salespeople. The usual reaction is to run over the obstacle and say it's not an issue. This can create resistance. Another approach is to acknowledge the obstacle and ask if it's a deal killer. If it is, better to know early than to talk the prospect out of their objection and sow the seeds of resentment and disappointment later. If the obstacle is not a deal killer, ask the prospect why they don't act if the obstacle is not important. Now you're helping the prospect learn about themselves and their situation without giving them what they asked for. That's a greater act of love than if you had been able to remove the obstacle that wasn't very important. Teaching a prospect to overlook their own bias may give them the courage to commit to what they know they should do. If your product or service has real value and is worth more than what people pay for it, every sale to someone who needs it is an act of love. That's a great way to become rich.

Nothing is less productive than having the same argument over and over, with no changes or new information. At home and at work, arguments should be productive. Understanding needs to grow. New information needs to be shared. New ideas need to be generated and new solutions proposed. Productive argument is not about winning; it's about evolving. You can improve the quality of an argument by reframing the argument to be about something bigger than the people arguing. Make the argument about customers and commitment to improvement and do it sincerely. What will make us better? What will help customers the most? Pretending to make an argument about something bigger when you really just want to win the argument is devious and sinful. Don't just try to win; try to get smarter.

Your Organization

Healthy conflict happens when people agree on goals but differ on means. When you agree on goals, assign the objective to one person, and let them pursue the objective their own way. When everyone is committed to loving customers and improving at expressing that love, you have a foundation on which to build solid relationships, even with people you don't like. These relationships can be the best part of your work. People who you never thought could be your ally can become your ally when they see you're dedicated to getting the right thing done as efficiently as possible. If your goals are the same, you can disagree about means and still remain coordinated. Where there's no agreement about goals, efforts at coordination are futile.

Customer love and commitment to improvement are great values for any organization. Values are more important than goals. Goals change all the time; values should not change so easily. Falling short of goals is disappointing. Falling short of values is inevitable. We want to get better, but we never get perfect. "The more our soul is filled, the larger it becomes," says Montaigne. Talk to customers all the time. Study them and listen to them. They're your children; give of yourself and be humble like a good parent.

Chapter in a Chart: Carry the Messages of Customer Love and Commitment to Improvement to Everyone You Meet

You carry the message when you ... ➡	You lose the message when you ...
Love customers by example.	Complain about customers or criticize them unconstructively.
Create a story that's about more than money.	Measure everything by activity or gain.
Praise people in public.	Harp on failure or don't celebrate success.
Admonish people in private.	Embarrass someone.
Avoid fights and blame.	Engage in conflict for conflict's sake.

Why it matters	➤➤ ➤ What to do about it
Everyone hates a hypocrite. If you talk about love, you have to show it. It's easier than you might think.	Express love in lots of small ways rather than with big gestures. Thank-you notes still mean a lot. Receiving them by surface mail means even more.
People need to know their work matters. For many people, knowing their work matters is worth a lot more than a cost-of-living raise.	Write a formal success story or testimonial for each outstanding customer success. Not all customers will agree to them, but you can never have enough, and they are useful, even if you don't share them outside your organization.
Well-placed criticism from someone who is free with praise has a greater effect on changing behavior than criticism from someone who is always critical.	Acknowledge small wins to yourself and others every day. Some days just persisting is a victory.
People don't forget being shamed, and they don't always get over it either. Why would you intentionally make someone weaker?	If you respectfully correct someone in a straightforward way and give them an idea of what the desired behavior is, you will become their teacher.
Winning will not make you wiser or happier in the long run. The euphoria of winning always dies.	Define winning for yourself, and no one can defeat you.

Practice Step 12

Hint: "Preventing something bad from happening is as good a way to promote customer love as doing something good."

The scenario:

You're working on a deadline when a salesperson comes into your office.

"You busy?" the salesperson asks. "Do you have some pictures of the winter release? I have a prospect who wants to see them." You're at a bit of a loss since the winter release is nine months away.

"What does your prospect need?" you ask because you need more information before you can appropriately react.

"My prospect wants to know more about the double-clone recycler," the salesperson says. "They're not going to implement until winter, so it doesn't matter that it isn't built yet."

You've heard about the double-clone recycler, and it's supposed to be a big strategic improvement. It's also just talk right now.

How should you respond?

If you want to say ...

- "Why do they want to know about the double-clone recycler?" go to page 263.

- "We can't commit to details about a release that far out," go to page 261.

"WE CAN'T COMMIT TO DETAILS ABOUT A RELEASE THAT FAR OUT."

"It's not a commitment," answers the salesperson. "They aren't implementing until the winter. Anyway, if you don't have anything, can we just whip something together for me to show them? Everybody's talking about the double-clone recycler, so we need this stuff now. If you don't, can you give me a template so I can put something together?"

How should you respond?

If you want to say ...

⊛ "I can't give you a template so you can make something up about a release that's not even defined," go to page 269.

⊛ "Have you talked to product management?" go to page 265.

"WHY DO THEY WANT TO KNOW ABOUT THE DOUBLE-CLONE RECYCLER?"

"Because you have to sell the sizzle!" says the salesperson. "Anyway, they don't know about the double-clone recycler yet, but I need something to get them excited, and the double-clone recycler is super cool."

How should you respond?

If you want to say ...

- "Have you talked to product management?" go to page 265.

- "Have you shared our new implementation process with them?" go to page 267.

"HAVE YOU TALKED TO PRODUCT MANAGEMENT?"

The salesperson sighs heavily.

"You're not helping. I'll do it myself." He leaves your office.

A few weeks go by, and you hear nothing more about it. Then one morning, you get a message from your supervisor: "Come see me as soon as you get in."

You slink into her office and sit down. She shuts the door.

"(Name of salesperson) created a document for a prospect about the double-clone recycler. They're very excited about it. They even signed. Now you have to call them and walk everything back."

Not a good outcome. How did this happen?

Someone came to you asking for help, and you didn't really help them. If you think it's not your job, you might be right, but it's become your job to fix it. If you had taken time to learn what the salesperson really needed, you might have been able to avoid this.

Is it wrong for salespeople to make things up about features that don't exist? Sure, but it's done to solve a problem—getting prospects to buy. Better to help solve the problem than act as if it's not your problem to solve.

Spread the gospel of customer love. It's not an act of love to get someone excited about something that doesn't exist, and it might not even be necessary to land the deal. You'll have to work to understand what the salesperson really needs and steer them toward a different action than talking about the double-clone recycler to a prospect who hasn't even heard of it.

If you want to try again, go to "Practice Step 12" on page 259.

"HAVE YOU SHARED OUR NEW IMPLEMENTATION PROCESS WITH THEM?"

"Implementation is like watching paint dry. I need sizzle," says the salesperson. "Besides, that thing has, like, one thousand words, and nobody reads. I need pictures," says the salesperson. "If you're too busy, can you give me a template, and I'll put something together myself?"

How should you respond?

If you want to say …

⚙ "Have you talked to product management?" go to page 265.

⚙ "You know what strategic accounts calls (name of the head of implementations)? The Closer," go to page 271.

"I CAN'T GIVE YOU A TEMPLATE SO YOU CAN MAKE SOMETHING UP ABOUT A RELEASE THAT'S NOT EVEN DEFINED."

The salesperson sighs heavily.

"You're not helping. I'll do it myself." He leaves your office.

A few weeks go by, and you hear nothing more about it. Then one morning, you get a message from your supervisor: "Come see me as soon as you get in."

You slink into her office and sit down. She shuts the door.

"(Name of salesperson) created a document for a prospect about the double-clone recycler. They're very excited about it. They even signed. Now you have to call them and walk everything back."

Not a good outcome. How did this happen?

Someone came to you asking for help, and you didn't really help them. If you think it's not your job, you might be right, but it's become your job to fix it. If you had taken time to learn what the salesperson really needed, you might have been able to avoid this.

Is it wrong for salespeople to make things up about features that don't exist? Sure, but it's done to solve a problem—getting prospects to buy. Better to help solve the problem than act as if it's not your problem to solve.

Spread the gospel of customer love. It's not an act of love to get someone excited about something that doesn't exist, and it might not even be necessary to land the deal. You'll have to work to understand what the salesperson really needs and steer them toward a different action than talking about the double-clone recycler to a prospect who hasn't even heard of it.

If you want to try again, go to "Practice Step 12" on page 259.

"YOU KNOW WHAT STRATEGIC ACCOUNTS CALLS (NAME OF THE HEAD OF IMPLEMENTATIONS)? 'THE CLOSER.'"

"Really? 'The Closer'?" The salesperson says. "I love that."

"Absolutely. Get him talking about implementation, and it's like he's already sold."

You forward the salesperson the new implementation guide, and he sends it on to the client.

A few weeks later, you get a note from the salesperson:

"Thanks for your help. My prospect geeked out on the guide. I talked to (name of the head of implementations). She said nobody has ever called her 'The Closer' to her face, but she loves it! She's joining me on the final presentation to the buying committee. We're going to focus on how our implementation is the best in the business. Fingers crossed! Thanks again!"

You succeeded in this scenario by demonstrating the values of "Step 11: Improve Your Insight through Contact with Customers, Colleagues, and People You Admire" and "Step 12: Carry the Messages of Customer Love and Commitment to Improvement to Everyone You Meet."

Well done!

WHAT COMES NEXT

All the steps are a lot of work, but the work is worth it. The next chapter proves why the work is worth it by creating a vision for you.

BEFORE

AFTER

CONCLUSION

A Vision for You

Dare to be wise! Begin!
The man who would reform, but hesitates, is kin
Unto the boor who waits until the stream is gone;
But ever flow the stream, and ever will flow on.
—HORACE AS QUOTED BY MONTAIGNE

'What do I know?' I know I'm hungry. And I could use a scratch.
—MONTAIGNE AS QUOTED BY MARGARET THE PUG

Living virtuously gives us the power to match calamity with serenity. Difficult things will happen to all of us; notably, we will all die, and we'll see people we love get sick and die. Virtue means we don't have to live in fear of these things. Hard things may try us, but they don't have to break us. Even death does not have to break us if we live our lives so people who know us will miss us.[8] A lot more people will miss Bill Gates and Oprah Winfrey than will ever miss me, but our deaths are equal. We each have only one life to give up; death is the great

---

8   "If you have made your profit of life, you have had your fill of it; go your way satisfied: 'Why, like a well-filled guest, not leave the feast of life?'" — Montaigne, quoting Lucretius

equalizer.[9] I know a man who has spent his entire adult life in prison, over forty years, most of it on death row. Prison has warped him, though he wasn't well when he arrived there, but it has not broken him. He wants company. He wants conversation like us all. I don't know positively that he did the things that he's convicted of; he may have. I do know that he's done some admirable things since being in prison, like writing a book, pursuing art, and educating himself. It's possible for the very lowest of us to achieve some measure of virtue, and it's possible for the most privileged and famous to be without any virtue. That's why I love virtue so much.

For many people, work is a series of disappointments and frustrations. What's worse, we often feel guilty about being unfulfilled by work since so much of what we hear is how fulfilling work should be. I think we have work all wrong. Work is not the job you get paid to do; though that's a small part of work. Work is your life. We all work for ourselves. You get to decide what success means. Define fortune in your own way, and choose your own path to fortune. For me fortune is happiness and virtue, and I find them mostly as a husband and a father and a writer. My consulting practice is wonderful too, because I meet new people and help them. Fortune for you might be riches and fame, or to suffer for a cause you believe in, or pleasure. How you define fortune is less important than making a deliberate choice and then reflecting on that choice often. I had a friend as a kid who had two ambitions: to own a Rolex and to drive a Porsche. He worked thirteen-hour days for slightly more than minimum wage until he could buy his Rolex. He was about eighteen and had knocked off one of his two life's ambitions. I could argue with the worthiness of his objectives, but he had them and knew what they were, and that was more than I had. His Rolex also seemed to make him genuinely

---

9   "All things, their life being done, will follow you." — Montaigne, quoting Lucretius

happy, though I think it was the "I wanted this and worked hard to get it" that the watch symbolized and less the watch itself. By working hard to afford something expensive, my friend stumbled into a number of virtues, like moderation and friendliness and wittiness. Who are any of us to judge another person's ambitions, including our own? As Montaigne says, "Only the fools are certain and assured."

> Who are any of us to judge another person's ambitions, including our own?

I knew I loved Anna soon after we started dating. On paper, everything about our relationship was wrong. She was eight years older than me. She had a good job, and I was in college. We were different religions. I had depression and was a recovering alcoholic. She was my first serious relationship sober. We moved in together after I graduated as a step toward getting married. Then one day I went to lunch with some older friends, and they all said how relationships between older women and younger men rarely work out, so I went home and told Anna that I'd been thinking about asking her to marry me, but I'd changed my mind. This ranks high among the dumbest things I've ever said. I actually thought Anna would be grateful to hear I'd been thinking about asking her to marry me. So here's my vision for you: you never have to be as stupid as I was. I said that stupid thing because I was not practicing these principles. I was looking for another person to validate my fear and selfishness. Since I started living by these principles—thinking about what I can do for others, listening to understand and not speaking to be understood, mediating, taking a regular inventory—I've never been happier or made more money with less effort. Discipline has transformed my life—the discipline of love. I live in a beautiful home Anna created, I have three children whom I love and enjoy and who love and enjoy me, and I have a business I'm proud of that gives me everything I need and most of what I want. It didn't happen only because of luck, though every accomplished person has some degree of luck. Oprah Winfrey is lucky she was born with so much talent; her character made it into a fortune.

Other than happiness and love, what does virtue buy you? I like Aristotle's answer: the chance to be magnanimous. Bill Gates will not be remembered for cofounding Microsoft and creating one of the largest personal fortunes the world has ever seen; he's going to be remembered for spending his fortune to eliminate disease, and perhaps for some of the details that emerged during his divorce, which is pathetic. I am not one to condemn the public good someone does because of their private habits. As a kid I always rooted for Steve Jobs versus Bill Gates. Steve died too young for his life to have a third act; we'll never know if he would have achieved the magnanimity that Bill Gates has. Bill Gates the person will die like the rest of us, but his foundation can persist for hundreds of years. Its impact on people not yet born may be profound.[10] Without great public character, Bill Gates would be just another rich guy. (His private character is a different thing altogether. It's not easy to live a good life in a palace.) Character matters, and character is the sum of our virtues and our vices. Wealth is just a condition. Our character is our true legacy, and it has the most lasting impact on those who know us best.

Aristotle felt the greatest good we can seek is honor, since honor is the greatest nonmaterial thing anyone can have. I disagree with Aristotle about honor.[11] Honor is the esteem of others; I'm not

---

10 "Our lives we borrow from each other ... and men, like runners, pass along the torch of life." — Lucretius, as quoted by Montaigne

11 Montaigne wasn't much for honor and glory either: "Of all the illusions of the world, the most universal is concern for reputation and glory, which we embrace to the point of giving up riches, rest, life, and health, which are real and fruitful goods, to follow that vain phantom and mere sound that has neither body nor substance."

interested. I care about my honor to myself. Let's consider Jesus as a man for a moment, putting aside any thoughts of his divinity or nondivinity. Born poor and in an obscure town, Jesus took on the Roman Empire and the society he was born into to proclaim a new way founded on love and mercy and the equality of all people. Love, mercy, and equality were not popular ideas among the powerful. Jesus accepted death rather than renounce his ideals, and I am unworthy to kiss his sandal, but he would have accepted me anyway because that's the kind of guy he was. Jesus's example inspired a moral code that has undeniably improved the lot of humanity, even if the institutions formed to advance (or exploit?) his teaching have had a less than positive impact on the world. Many people would say they love Jesus more than their spouse or their children or themselves. The accomplishment seems more remarkable to me if Jesus is not God. I love ethics; I'm less enthusiastic about religion. The reality or nonreality of God will take care of itself. I have my life to live. I need to live it ethically if I want to enjoy it.

Marie Curie and Aristotle are vastly more consequential than I am, but we are not different animals. My life is more consequential to people who love me than either of their lives. My contributions to the betterment of humanity are puny. I don't despise myself for it. There are always superheroes among us, cleverer than mortals, enduring great adversities, and living far outside the bounds of ordinary morality. I am not one of them, but I am on my way to becoming enough. I encourage you to join me and pursue a life of virtue, but if you prefer Rolexes and Porsches, that's OK too. You might end up at virtue anyway.

I got sober at twenty-one. For the first thirty years of my career, I told almost no one I was in recovery. I was afraid of how people would react. Now I've found my fortune, and I'm not afraid anymore.

Acknowledgments

Bill Engel, for introducing me to Montaigne. Michael Sousa, for getting *Fortune's Path* started and for being a supportive reader. Josh Oakes, for the idea to bang out one chapter for each step. Michael and Pam Sheridan, for many things, but particularly for telling me that if I wrote one thousand words a day for thirty days, at the end of thirty days I'd have something that can become a book. Ben Kettle, for being a sounding board and encouraging me to stay with it. Christy Frink and Michelle Egly, for helping me commit to what I love about business. Bill Horne, for believing in *Fortune's Path*. Joe Ingle for the opportunity to learn. Lola White O'Hara, for the example. My father, Eugene A. Noser Jr., and my wife, Anna Grimes, for everything and more; my children; and of course, Margaret, my inspiration and my Buddha.

Keep in Touch

It's wonderful to hear from readers, and we'd love to hear from you, especially if it's to say what we could do better. Drop us a line at hello@fortunespath.com. You can also subscribe to our newsletter at www.fortunespath.com or listen to our podcast, *Fortune's Path with Tom Noser*, on Apple, Spotify, or wherever you get your podcasts.

If you want to send something to Margaret, she prefers chicken flavor, and her favorite place to be scratched is behind the ears.

Appendix

12 Steps of Product Management, and the Product Is You

The step is ... ➡	The step isn't ...
1. Identify what you can and can't control.	Giving up and saying, "We're all just where we should be."
2. Improve the things you can control, and accept the things you can't.	An excuse to be lazy.
3. Make a decision to love your customers.	A guarantee of love in return.
4. Decide what kind of leader you want to be.	An attack on people who don't want to lead others.
5. Make an inventory of your character.	A list of your faults.
6. Share your inventory with a trusted friend.	A tell-all biography.

Why it matters ⬸ ➡	What to do about it
You have to understand what you can and cannot control to succeed and be happy.	Take collaboration seriously. Seek and give input freely. I doubt that all of Napoleon's men thought invading Russia was a great idea.
You can control more than you think, but you're trying to control the wrong things.	Take pride in your professionalism. When you feel down, read your résumé. Look at your LinkedIn connections. Pull up some work you're proud of. Call somebody who loves you.
If you love everyone, even people you don't like, you will acquire power and be happy.	Seek to know what's real. Don't overvalue yourself, your product, or your people, and don't undervalue them either. This is the work of a lifetime.
You can decide what kind of leader to be, and you can decide not to be a leader at all. You can control your behavior, but you can't control your results.	We all have anxiety and pain. You give up the right to share yours in public when you become a leader. Find a group of confidants you can share openly with and get whatever help you need.
You can change your character, and good character leads to a good life.	Don't become a leader to make yourself happy. Become a leader to serve others—which will make you happy—and to accumulate power.
You need other people to learn what will make you happy.	Do more of what you're good at. Seek honest feedback about it. Believe what the people who love you say. Put in the work to get better.

12 Steps of Product Management, and the Product Is You

The step is ... ➡	The step isn't ...
7. Embrace your character—all of it.	A blank check to be rude and selfish.
8. Make a list of all the people around you who can help you succeed.	A target market list.
9. Speak with all the people on your list to learn what they need to succeed.	Selling.
10. Take a daily inventory.	A to-do list.
11. Improve your insight through contact with customers, colleagues, and people you admire.	Only read to confirm your current opinions.
12. Carry the messages of customer love and commitment to improvement to everyone you meet.	Pump yourself and your customers with hot air.

Why it matters	→	What to do about it
You can only shape your character and improve it if you embrace all of it, virtues and vices, because vices are just over- or underdeveloped virtues.		Don't let your intelligence or expertise get in the way of growing wise. Remind yourself daily that even the people you know well are a mystery, often to themselves. Accept people as they are, including yourself.
More people love you than you know, including people you haven't met yet, and all of them can help you.		Frequently update your list of people who can help you succeed. Your list should always be growing. Reading it can be encouraging in dark times.
You can get more from someone by listening to them than by talking to them.		Follow up on the things people tell you they need. Give status updates, even if the update is "I haven't gotten to it yet." Anticipate needs where you can.
Being busy and making progress are very different. "I am happier today than I was before" is progress. Busyness is distraction.		Make a deliberate choice. Don't stumble into a life you don't want, and if you do, change it.
Anyone can be your teacher. Even fools are right sometimes.		When you talk to customers, keep the conversation about them. Don't talk about your company or your products unless you're asked.
Preventing something bad from happening is as good a way to promote customer love as doing something good.		Acknowledge small wins to yourself and others every day. Some days just persisting is a victory.

The Saint Francis Prayer

Lord, make me an instrument of your peace.

Where there is hatred, let me bring love.

Where there is offense, let me bring pardon.

Where there is discord, let me bring union.

Where there is error, let me bring truth.

Where there is doubt, let me bring faith.

Where there is despair, let me bring hope.

Where there is darkness, let me bring your light.

Where there is sadness, let me bring joy.

O master, let me not seek as much

To be consoled as to console,

To be understood as to understand,

To be loved as to love,

For it is in giving that one receives,

It is in self-forgetting that one finds,

It is in pardoning that one is pardoned,

It is in dying that one is raised to eternal life.